My Dear Boy

Rev. Arthur Bell Nicholls, B.A.
Taken about the time of his marriage to Mary Anna

My Dear Boy

The life of Arthur Bell Nicholls, B.A.

Husband of Charlotte Brontë

By

Margaret and Robert Cochrane

Highgate of Beverley

Highgate Publications (Beverley) Limited

1999

British Library Cataloguing in Publication Data.
A catalogue record for this book is available from the British Library.

© 1999 Margaret and Robert Cochrane

ISBN 1 902645 03 0

Published by

Highgate of Beverley

Highgate Publications (Beverley) Limited
24 Wylies Road, Beverley, HU17 7AP
Telephone (01482) 866826

Produced by

4 Newbegin, Lairgate, Beverley, HU17 8EG
Telephone (01482) 886017

Front Cover Picture: Rev. Arthur Bell Nicholls B.A. taken about the time of his marriage to Charlotte.
Courtesy of the Brontë Society

Contents

List of Illustrations

Acknowledgements

Whilst we have had help and assistance from many people and many sources, we should particularly like to thank John Markham for his advice and encouragement; the Library Staff of the Brontë Parsonage Museum for their patience and help during long hours of research. Mrs Bridie Mahon, for pointing us in the right directions; Valentine Trodd, local historian; Miss Valerie Landon, reminiscences of Cuba House; Rev. Wayne Carney, Rector of St Paul's, Banagher, and Mike Gorman, owner of The Hill House; Miss Jean Blackburn of Beverley for showing us the records of the Dawson/Eggleston family; Rev. Elizabeth Thomas, Vicar of St Paul's Church, Denholme Gate; Alan Humphries, Librarian, Thackray Medical Museum; and Manchester University Press, (see Glossary).

We also wish to acknowledge the many places where we pursued our research and, where appropriate, the permissions they have given to quote from their records:

Brontë Parsonage Museum
Ripon Diocese Archives, Ripon
Lichfield Diocesan Archives Lichfield
The Borthwick Institute, York
York Minster Library
Holy Trinity Church, Sunk Island
St Paul's Church Archives, Denholme Gate
St Paul's Church, Banagher
St Peter's Church , Kirk Smeaton
USPG Archives, London
Rhodes House, Oxford
The Brotherton Collection, Brotherton Library, Leeds
    University, Leeds
Bodleian Library, Oxford
John Murray (Smith Elder & Co archives)
Pierpont Morgan Library, New York, USA

Berg Collection of English and American Literature, The New York Public Library, Astor, Lennox and Tilden Foundations.

The Carl H. Pforzheimer Collection of Shelley and his Circle. The New York Public Library, Astor, Lennox and Tilden Foundations.

West Riding Archives: Wakefield, Leeds, Bradford and Halifax; Reference and Local History departments of Public Libraries at Keighley, Bradford, Leeds, Halifax, Kingston upon Hull and Beverley.

Gawthorpe Hall

In Wales: Gwynedd Archives Service, Conway; Bangor and Holyhead Public Libraries.

In Ireland: General Register Office, Dublin; Genealogical Office, Dublin; Trinity College Library, Dublin; The National Maritime Museum, Dun Laoghaire; Banagher Public Library.

Preface

Arthur Bell Nicholls is, with Aunt Branwell, the unsung member of the Brontë circle. He was a part of Charlotte's life for its last ten years, and knew all the Brontë children who survived infancy. Above all, he made the last months of Charlotte's life extremely happy, and was a fierce and true guardian of her memory after her death.

It is easy to quote Charlotte in the early years of her acquaintance with him saying less than complimentary things about his rigid beliefs and stiffness of demeanour. More significant, to my mind, are the moments when she is away from Haworth and writes to her father wishing that Mr Nicholls could have seen this or the other thing. He was more often in her mind than Charlotte realized, reminding one of Jane Austen's Emma, who is quite unaware how large Mr Knightley looms in her thoughts. Most significant of all, when she brings him in at the end of *Shirley,* the fun she makes of him is extremely affectionate – which he recognised by his roars of appreciative laughter. There were not many curates with whom Charlotte was on such terms that she could make affectionate fun of them – still fewer that she would have wanted to.

Mr Nicholl's reserve was such, and his fierce protectiveness of his and Charlotte's privacy was such, that we have tended till now to see him through other people's eyes, notably Mr Brontë's at the time of his fierce opposition to the marriage, Ellen's and Mrs Gaskell's. All of them in their different ways were proud of Charlotte's fame and wished to have her genius and self-sacrifice more widely known and celebrated. To Arthur Bell Nicholls, understandably, she was his wife, the proudest and most sacred part of his private life. He defended her like a lion when her veracity was called in question, as it was over Cowan Bridge School, and he delighted in her fame, authorising the publication of *The Professor* and other works by her and her sisters. But beyond that he felt the public had no right to pry, and, though this attitude is at odds with our own prying age, his feelings are honourable and probably in tune with Charlotte's own wishes.

It is good, though, that at last an attempt is being made to do justice to a prickly, difficult but warm and human man. Margaret and Robert Cochrane's book will find a ready and interested audience.

Robert Barnard
(Chairman, The Brontë Society)

Early Life and Training

'Charlotte, – Charlotte –'[1]
The nurse in attendance heard the whisper from the old man in the bed, and turned in time to see his eyes close peacefully, his last sight on earth the face in the portrait on his bed-side table. So, on a December day in 1906, in The Hill House, Banagher, Ireland, died Charlotte Brontë's 'dear boy', the husband she had learned to love and with whom she had had so little time.[2] In spite of age and remarriage, Arthur Bell Nicholls never stopped loving her. He had left Haworth in 1861 to return to Ireland bringing with him as many mementoes of Charlotte as he could, and had turned his house into a shrine to her memory. Of her were his last conscious thoughts.

His coffin was placed in the drawing room under her portrait until the funeral. He was buried in the churchyard at Banagher, quite near to the house, just a few weeks before his eighty-eighth birthday.

When Arthur died on 3rd December 1906, Edward VII was on the throne and the British Empire was at its zenith. The railway system was fully developed; motor cars were appearing on the roads; the electric light bulb, telephone and radio had all been invented; the first men had flown. It was a far cry from the state of the Nation at his birth in 1819: then George III was still King, although at that time his son was Regent; Queen Victoria was yet to be born. It was less than four years since the Battle of Waterloo; the navy was still relying on its 'wooden walls'; stage coaches were the main form of public transport; industrialisation was rapidly taking place but there was still a long way to go to reach the scale and variety of production of the later 19th century.

In between these two dates, the country had been involved in two major wars and numerous minor ones; Queen Victoria had started and finished her triumphant reign and Ireland had suffered the tragedy of the potato famine. Yet somehow Arthur seems strangely aloof from all this, the one great passionate feeling of his life being his love of, and marriage, to Charlotte Brontë.

Born on January 6th, 1819, Arthur was the fourth son in a family of ten children.[3] His father, William, was a small farmer at Killead, in the townland of Tully, Co. Antrim. In common with Mr Brontë he spelled his name in a variety of ways – Nichols, Nickles or Nicholls. The family were Presbyterian, of Scottish descent, who had settled in Ireland in the 1620s.[4]

Arthur's mother, Margaret Nicholls, née Bell, was also of a Scottish family but, unlike her husband's, her family belonged to the Established Church.[5] Their home was at Glenavy, a parish nearby, where her brother Alan was Curate. The same year Arthur was born, Rev. Alan Bell met and married a charming, attractive, 18-year-old bride, Harriette Lucinda Adamson. He was twelve years older than his wife but that did not prevent the marriage being very happy and successful – they produced nine children. Fortunately for Arthur, this family played a major part in his upbringing. Life on a small farm in Ireland in the early part of the 19th century cannot have been easy, especially when it had to support ten children and two adults but the Bells were able to help. In 1821 Rev., now Dr Bell, had bought the headmastership of the Royal Free School at Banagher on the Shannon from Thomas Morris and had moved into the imposing house which went with the position. Back at the Nicholls' farm the eldest two sons helped their father on the land and, in 1825, Arthur and his elder brother, Alan, were taken by Dr and Mrs Bell to Banagher to be brought up and educated: a relief for their parents, giving them more space, fewer mouths to feed and ensuring a good start in life for the boys.

The town of Banagher is situated almost in the centre of Ireland at a crossing of the River Shannon. At the time the Bells came there, it consisted of little more than a single street, with Georgian houses on either side, climbing uphill from the bridge to the Church. The school and Cuba Court, where Dr and Mrs Bell lived in some style, were a little way beyond this.

The Royal Free School had been founded by charter in 1628, with an income from lands confiscated from the Coughlans.[6] In 1818 Thomas Morris became headmaster and moved the school to Cuba Court, the property at that time owned by Dennis Bowes Daly, and, some three years later, had sold the headmastership to Dr Bell. The school itself was housed in a range of dormitories and classrooms behind the house.

Reached by an avenue of lime trees, the house had originally been built in 1730 for George Frazer, a former governor of Cuba, and from this had been named Cuba Court; locally, however, it was known as Cuba House.[7] It was a substantial building of two stories and a basement, both the west front, of five bays, and the south front, of seven bays, being decorated with break-front pediments.

What a mixture of emotions the two young boys must have felt as they approached the iron gates of the carriage drive – excitement, trepidation, curiosity, the first twinges of home sickness – not unlike modern day children newly arriving for their first days at boarding school. But this was better; after all, they were with family and they had each other for comfort. The journey had been long and arduous – well over a hundred miles by coach along the bumpy roads – but when they saw the house they were to live in it must have seemed worth-while.

At this time, Arthur was seven-years-old and Alan nine. The Bells had just one child, a year-old son, also named Alan, like his cousin and his father, which must have caused some confusion. As the years went by and the size of the family increased, so did Dr Bell's wealth. He invested in land: buying it, farming it and letting it. The family wanted for nothing and all the children grew up cultured, well educated and kind. Aunt Harriet was sensible and loving. She had loyal servants, and the big house with its spacious rooms, handsome furniture and warm turf fires was a gracious and happy home. In this stable environment Arthur's childhood made its natural, even progress.

The contrast between this and the life of nine-year-old Charlotte Brontë growing up at Haworth could not have been greater. She had just passed through one of the worst and most traumatic periods of her life, the deaths of her mother and her two older sisters, Maria and Elizabeth. Her distressing time at the notorious Cowan Bridge School was still fresh in her mind and her unhappy memories were to haunt her throughout her life. She turned to her fantasy world for comfort. Her only playmates were her remaining sisters and brother: not for her the normal rough and tumble of the world outside. The family was short of money, her father sad and worried. She learned to show a calm exterior, not to expect too much from life. Her childhood was over, just as Arthur's was blossoming .

At the Royal School Arthur and his brother received a thorough classical education with boys of their own age and interests. Their spare time was spent in the beautiful countryside around Banagher. The family lived the life of country gentlefolk and doubtless they took part in the usual country pursuits like picnics on the river, fishing, large family gatherings, gardening, walking and riding. The Bells were great animal lovers and kept pet dogs. Arthur, who loved dogs all his life, also liked the wild animals such as squirrels that abounded in the area. He never lost his love of the open air and nature.

In reality, if not officially, the boys were adopted by their uncle and aunt and, although their father was a Presbyterian, they were brought up in the doctrines of the then United Church of England and Ireland. They lived with their growing number of cousins as part of one family. Arthur was very proud of his descent from the Bells on his mother's side of the family and later drew up an elaborate Bell family tree, detailing their descent from Michael Bell, a colonel who came over with King William in 1690.

In 1830, when Arthur was twelve, his mother died on the family farm. As the journey from Killead to Banagher was difficult in those pre-railway days it is unlikely they would be able to get there in time to attend the funeral. That same year Mary Anna was born, the fifth of the Bell's nine children. As she grew older, she became Arthur's favourite cousin.

Dr Bell saw to it that both Alan and Arthur went to university to complete their education. Arthur was admitted to Trinity College, Dublin, on July 4th, 1836, and matriculated in January, 1837; that is to say, he was enrolled having the required qualifications to study there for a degree. Trinity College had been founded in 1592 by Elizabeth I on the site of the former Priory of All Hallows which had been dissolved by her father, Henry VIII. It was very much a Protestant foundation aimed to further the Reformation and help convert the Irish to Protestantism. Roman Catholics were not admitted until 1873 and then, fearing the pervasive influence of this seat of Protestant learning, the Catholic Church issued its own ban on its members attending, which remained in force until as recently as 1970. When Arthur was up at University in the early 1840s, Trinity College, Dublin, was, along with Oxford and Cambridge, one of the three major sources of clergy for the Established Church.

Most of the University was rebuilt in the 18th century and extended over the following years. The west front was built in the 1750s and the Public Theatre, which was the examination hall, in the 1780s. It would be with these buildings that Arthur was familiar. Arthur attended University as a 'pensioner': his expenses, his 'commons', were paid for by his uncle. This is in contrast to Patrick Brontë who attended Cambridge as a 'sizar': some of his fees were paid by benefactors (including William Wilberforce) but he had to perform menial duties to make up the full amount. University in those days was a leisurely business and Arthur was there seven years. However, this was at a time of great turmoil within the Church over the merits or demerits of Evangelicalism as opposed to the High Church approach.

In the early 19th century, Evangelicalism was in the ascendancy in the Church. That is to say, preaching and teaching were based primarily on the gospels. The Evangelicals laid stress on faith, personal conversion and atonement, giving less importance to the Eucharist and the following of traditions. They believed strongly in social reform and missionary work: many of them were involved in those movements which led to the Factory Acts and the abolition of slavery. Their views were broadly similar to those of the Methodists but they preferred to remain within the Church of England and inevitably there was some lack of harmony between Evangelicals and those with High Church sympathies.

In 1833 the difference between the two wings of the Church was given more form when Rev. John Keble preached a sermon on *National Apostasy* in Oxford and this was followed by publication of *Tracts for the Times,* by Rev. John Henry Newman. They called for a higher standard of piety, worship and devotion, stressed the importance of the Apostolic succession of the clergy, and insisted that salvation was only possible through the sacraments. This faction of the Church became known as the Oxford (or the Tractarian) Movement.

The polarisation caused by these philosophies led to religious ferment in Oxford: this rapidly spread to theological colleges and throughout the Church. In 1845 the Tractarian movement received a shock when Newman joined the Roman Catholic Church but quickly re-formed under the leadership of Rev. Edward Bouverie Pusey, Professor of Hebrew at Oxford, and persons of High Church leanings became known as Puseyites, the epithet often used by Evangelicals in a disparaging way.

Even if young men got up to their usual student tricks, since most were intending to go into the Church, by the time they left they would have absorbed an air of gravity. Religious politics were discussed passionately at Trinity College and it was here Arthur developed his bias towards High Church Anglicanism. In addition to his bachelor's degree, Arthur obtained the Divinity Testimonium which was essential if he was to become a clergyman. So in 1844 he came out into the world, sombre, grave, reticent and perhaps a little shy, but in religion insistent on the proper observance of the traditions and liturgy of the Church.

No satisfactory explanation has so far been offered as to how Arthur, whose home was in the centre of Ireland, ended up in the centre of England. There were, of course, many more positions for curates in England: the majority of these were better paid and offered more opportunities for preferment than those in Ireland and, as a result, it was quite common for Irishmen to seek employment in the Church in England – indeed Patrick, himself, was Irish. However, he had come from a very different strata of society, by a different route, and from a different university.

There was a strong clerical grapevine and Patrick Brontë would have written to all his fellow parsons and friends in an endeavour to find a suitable curate. Similarly, Arthur would have used all means possible to learn of suitable curacies. Networking is nothing new. However, Patrick had already exhausted this source when Charlotte wrote to Ellen on 26th October, 1844: 'Mr Smith "Curate" is gone hence . . .' – she had a very low opinion of Smith which came out in *Shirley*, where he had been used as the pattern for Mr Malone. She went on to say in her letter, 'Nobody regrets him because nobody could attach themselves to one who could attach himself to nobody . . .'

Even so, with the multifarious duties of the parish and schools to perform, even an unlikable curate would be better than no curate at all. By now Mr Brontë would be getting desperate: no candidate was found in time for the ordination by the Bishop of Ripon, held in Lent. The Bishop of Ripon's next ordination was not until the autumn. It was almost a year since Arthur had obtained his degree. From his point of view it was important that he found an incumbent willing to nominate him as his curate, for such a nomination was required before he could put his name forward for Ordination.

Although the 'grapevine' might work in a number of cases it could not be relied upon to be 100% effective. No previous reference has been made to other modern means, such as advertising. There was published, throughout most of the 19th century, *The Ecclesiastical Gazette*, subtitled *Monthly Register of the affairs of the Church of England and of its Religious Societies and Institutions*.[8] This contained articles of interest to the clergy, reports from bodies such as the National Society (schools), H.M. Commissioners for New Churches and the missionary societies such as The United Society for the Propagation of the Gospel (U.S.P.G.). It contained reports of legislation or legal cases affecting the Church or particular parishes and also details of when the Bishops' Ordinations were to be held, preferments, and deaths.

The second part consisted of advertisements for curates and prospective curates seeking posts, incumbents wanting curates, incumbents wishing to exchange livings, sale of advowsons and similar transactions. Some of these expressed preferences for High or Low Church views: 'He must be of evangelical sentiments', 'A priest of Anglo-Catholic principles', 'of old Church of England principles', 'Evangelical not Tractarian' or 'moderate High Church principles'. A similar collection of offers and requests for teachers, tutors and governesses was followed by what can only be described as the vicars' version of *Exchange and Mart*. Such items were offered as: church barrel and finger organs, tooth powder and brushes, altar cloths, vicars wanting lodgers (female), insurances, loans, organs and apollonicons, second-hand sounding boards, hermetically sealed commode pail (guaranteed odourless), silk for robes, spectacle lenses, second-hand furniture, hunting and ladies' saddles, cloth for suits, and medicines. This section ended with several pages advertising the sale of sermons, hymns, tracts and books.

Advertisements, both those seeking, and those offering, employment, often used accommodation addresses and did not mention the parties by name. Although there were a number which could have related to Mr Nicholls, there was only one which might relate to Haworth:

'November 1844
A Title for Orders may be heard of in the West Riding of Yorkshire. Apply to Mr Thomas Harrison, Bookseller and Publisher, 153 Briggate, Leeds.'

This seems reminiscent of Mr Brontë's terse style! Nicholls graduated in February 1844 and one very full advertisement in 1844 looks like that of a new graduate:

'August, 1844
Title for Orders wanted by an A.B. of Trinity College
Dublin with high testimonials, a curacy with title. He
has no objection to a populous parish and would
undertake to instruct one or two lads over 12 years of
age for 3 hours a day in classics & mathematics, to
which he is fully competent, having taken honours in
College on several occasions. In the latter case the
stipend is expected to be commensurate .
Reply by letter prepaid, stating particulars to GWS,
Post Office, Paradise Row, Chelsea.'

Other advertisements are briefer but some specify in time for
particular Ordinations. In 1845, after holding an Ordination in
Lent, the Bishop of Ripon was not holding another until
September. Other Bishops were holding Ordinations on Trinity
Sunday, 18th May, 1845. Later advertisements by graduates
were briefer and more pointed:

'January, 1845.
Wanted by a Graduate of Trinity College, Dublin, of
moderate Church views, a title to orders with curacy. If
neighbourhood be good stipend no object. The South of
England would be preferred. Address (prepaid) A. B.
Rumford St. Liverpool.'

'February, 1845.
Curacy – wanted a Title for Orders and curacy by a
graduate now reading with a clergyman, on Trinity
Sunday next, in the Diocese of Lincoln or Peterboro.
Satisfactory testimonials can be produced. Address
(Prepaid) to A.M. at Mrs Leary's Newspaper Office,
Duke St., St James, London.'

'March, 1845.
Title for Orders wanted by a B.A. of Trinity College,
Dublin whose testimonials are in order, and whose
references will be found satisfactory. A Title for Orders
in the Diocese of Chester for the Trinity Sunday
Ordination. Letters addressed (prepaid) to AB at Mrs
Leary's Newspaper Agent, 22 Duke St., St James.'

It is likely that by some such means Nicholls got in touch with
Mr Brontë and it is most probable that he would have visited

Haworth early in 1845, to discuss the position with him, before receiving Mr Brontë's written nomination. Following this, either directly, or through his superior, the Vicar of Bradford, Mr Brontë would have had to get in touch with the Bishop of Ripon and ask that, in view of the urgency, arrangements be made for Nicholls to be ordained by another Bishop instead of waiting for the next Ordination in Ripon in the Autumn.

The Church even in those days was quite bureaucratic. The candidate had to send with his request for Ordination: a certificate of baptism; a testimonial from three beneficed clergymen, which in addition had to confirm that he had not at any time 'held, written or taught any thing contrary to the doctrine or discipline of the United Church of England and Ireland'; a letter from the Incumbent and a Churchwarden of his Parish Church confirming that his request for Ordination had been read out, asking if there was any 'just cause or impediment for which he might not be admitted' – rather like the marriage service; his College references and, in the case of graduates from Trinity, his Divinity Testimonium; and, lastly, his proposed appointment, in this case the nomination as Curate of Haworth by Patrick Brontë.

Unfortunately, unlike those of most other clergy, Nicholls' Ordination papers are not in either the Ripon or Lichfield Archives as these could have provided a wealth of detail. However, in the Bishop's Act book at Ripon is a record of the Bishop granting letters dimissory (authorisation) to Nicholls and a fellow candidate, James Arrowsmith, to be ordained at Lichfield.

He was ordained Deacon by the Rt. Rev. John (Lonsdale), Lord Bishop of Lichfield, along with ten other candidates for the Diaconate and seventeen for Priesthood, at a general ordination held in the Cathedral Church of Lichfield on Trinity Sunday, 18th May, 1845. Subsequently the Bishop of Ripon, Dr Longley, commissioned the Vicar of Bradford, Rev. William Scoresby, to license Arthur to the Curacy of the Church at Haworth. This he did on 5th June, and it was entered in the Curate's Licence Book at Ripon, on 9th June, 1845.

Arrival at Haworth

Although the moors were at its back, Haworth, in the mid-19th century, was a busy, industrial community, looking down the valley towards the towns rather than to the country. Most people were employed at a number of large textile mills, but some wool-combing and weaving was still done at home. The houses were crowded together and, for most, living conditions were poor. Visitors noted the smoky chimneys, mill-hands going to dinner clattering down sidewalks in wooden clogs, and, in the houses, oatbread drying on racks hung from the ceilings. The railway had reached Keighley, three to four miles away, in 1847 and through Leeds was connected to the growing national network. The Vicar of Bradford considered it 'a very wild and rough part', with a 'rude dissenting population'. This description may owe something to the independence of the local churchwardens, who had caused successive Vicars problems, as there seems little in the records to show Haworth as more unruly than anywhere else at that time.

On a spring day in May, 1845, the Rev. Arthur Bell Nicholls, T.C.D., B.A., arrived in Haworth, much to the relief of Patrick Brontë, whose rapidly failing eyesight, due to the thickening of his cataracts, was causing concern to all his family. Could he have seen his new curate properly, he would have observed that he was a well-built, good looking young man, about 5 ft 10 ins in height with long full sideburns, as was then fashionable, and hair 'as black as coil'[1]. He could tell more by the voice which was deep and unusually rich. At the age of 27 Arthur took his first appointment seriously and behaved with gravity, as befitted a man of the cloth. Arrangements had been made for him to lodge just down the lane with the sexton, John Brown, and his family. Brown was a stonemason and a great friend of Branwell Brontë. The cottage, built by John Brown himself, was called Sexton House, and John and Mary, his wife, occupied it with their daughters, Ann, Eliza, Tabitha, Mary and Hannah. Their eldest daughter, Martha, worked as a servant at the parsonage. It was inevitable that whatever happened there was soon known in Sexton House. The cottage adjoined the National School and was only a few yards from the Church, the two centres of his work. Arthur, who made something of a fetish of fresh air and exercise, was given his own room, which he also used as a study. He cut round holes in the door panel, saying he could not get a breath of air without them, much to his landlady's consternation.

Arthur found himself immediately set to work. He had arrived in Haworth within a week of his Ordination and conducted his first service the following Sunday, May 25th, 1845. He performed his first marriage three days later and his first funeral the day after that. Naturally , as a newcomer, he was the subject of much curious interest, not least from Charlotte Brontë. In a letter to Mrs Rand, a former teacher at Haworth National School, she wrote, 'Papa has got a new curate lately, a Mr Nicholls from Ireland – he did duty for the first time on Sunday – he appears a respectable young man, reads well and I hope will give satisfaction.'[2] He had made a favourable impression on one person at least. His life in Haworth was going to be very busy and he was to find that he earned every penny of his stipend of £90 per annum.

Patrick Brontë quickly realised he had a dedicated reliable and trustworthy helper. In the months that followed Arthur took over the majority of parish duties and got to know the other clergy in the district. Unfortunately Charlotte's view of him as a 'respectable young man' soon took a sharp knock. One day in June, when Arthur had held office for only a month, the three curates in the Haworth Parish, Joseph Grant of Oxenhope, James Bradley of Oakworth and Arthur himself 'dropped, or rather rushed unexpectedly, in to tea.' at the Parsonage.[3] Charlotte was hot and tired – it was Monday, baking day. They began 'glorifying themselves and abusing dissenters' in such a way that she lost her temper and gave them a sharp tongue lashing. It was such a shock coming from this normally quiet and shy woman that they were all, including her father, Patrick, struck dumb with amazement. But the damage had been done; these three confirmed her view that curates were the lowest form of life. Thereafter she treated Arthur coldly and politely and kept him at a distance. During his regular Monday evening visits to discuss parish matters with Patrick she kept out of the way in the drawing room.

Not that Arthur had much time to notice – he was being kept busy with work at the school each week-day, tutoring on

Saturday mornings at his lodgings to augment his meagre salary, and attending to all the parish duties that Mr Brontë found increasingly difficult to perform. He took over the completion of the arrangements for the Annual Sunday School Services in July and a special hymn sheet was printed by Robert Aked of Keighley.[4] The sermons at the afternoon and evening services were to be preached by visiting clergymen, the 2 p.m. service by Rev. Philip Eggleston, curate of Heptonstall, the next parish across the moors to the south of Haworth, and in the evening by Rev. William Scoresby, Vicar of Bradford. The visiting preachers were to be entertained at the Parsonage. Normally Charlotte acted as hostess on such occasions, but this time she was staying in Hathersage with Ellen Nussey, a friend from her school days. They had gone to visit Ellen's brother, Henry, who had recently been appointed Vicar, and to view the alterations he had made to his vicarage. Ellen, seemingly with little difficulty, persuaded Charlotte to stay another week, thus missing the Sunday School Service. Emily agreed with the proposal and she and Anne were left in charge of the entertaining.

The Rev. Philip Eggleston had come to Heptonstall, his first curacy, the year before. He came from East Yorkshire and had trained at the Clerical College of St Bees in Cumberland (Cumbria) and had been ordained deacon in January, 1844.[5] Although Eggleston was three years older than Arthur, they were in similar positions in semi-industrial parishes on either side of the moor and a friendship grew up which developed further when Philip moved to Keighley a year later. He had five sisters, one of whom, Emma, married James Dawson, a local farmer, at Rise in East Yorkshire. There is a strong tradition in the Dawson family that another sister, Margaret Eggleston, was at one time engaged to Arthur.[6]

Newly ordained curates usually stayed in their first appointment for two to three years and then looked to move on to a more advanced, more lucrative, position. If they were to get a parish of their own, it was considered preferable for the incumbent to be married. Happily this pressure coincided with a young man's natural instincts and many a young curate was actively seeking a wife. His choice was limited by income and the desire for an educated partner, often resulting in marriage to the daughter or sister of another clergyman. Margaret Eggleston was the same age as Arthur and it is more than likely they met. After her first initial good reaction, Charlotte did not speak well of her father's curate, which perhaps led him to look elsewhere. Or perhaps she did not speak well of him because he was already looking further afield than the Parsonage.

Whatever the truth about a possible engagement, nothing came of it, and Margaret Eggleston subsequently married Rev. Joseph Walker Jenkins, curate of Stanningley. He was the son of Rev. David Jenkins, the incumbent of Pudsey and an old friend of Patrick Brontë. He had followed Patrick as curate at Dewsbury; his daughter Harriet was at the Clergy School with Maria and Elizabeth Brontë and he had arranged through his brother, Rev. Evan Jenkins, Chaplain at Brussels, the introduction of the Brontës to the Pensionnat Heger. David Jenkins officiated at his son's wedding, which took place in May, 1848 at Philip Eggleston's new church, St Paul's, Denholme Gate.

The choice of the Rev. Dr Scoresby, Vicar of Bradford, to preach at the evening service was a good one from all points of view. At a difficult time in Scoresby's ministry, Patrick showed his support by the invitation: Arthur was able to meet his superior sociably at the Parsonage, and Scoresby himself was an interesting preacher, likely to attract a large congregation – no small consideration when there was to be a silver collection. When he came to preach at Haworth William Scoresby was 55 and shortly to retire.[7] He was the son of a whaling captain and first went to sea on his father's ship, to Greenland, at the age of ten. For the next 20 years he spent every summer in the Arctic and every winter at school in Whitby broadening his education, learning geometry, algebra, navigation, Latin, drawing and music. When he outgrew his school's teaching he enrolled at Edinburgh University, where he read natural history, mathematics, logic and anatomy. He made notes and drawings of his voyages and had some fascinating adventures. Always a religious man, he made sure his crew had a service on Sundays, preaching the sermon himself. He made sure his ships were clean and adequately provisioned and, due to his diligence, he never had a case of scurvy on any of his voyages. As a result of his scientific interests, he became a member of the British Association and gave lectures at the Royal Institution.

In 1825 at the age of 36 he was ordained a curate and commenced his career in the Church. When he was appointed Vicar of Bradford in 1839 he found himself in charge of a large, disorganised, understaffed and underfunded parish. Being responsible for paying his own curates he found he was left with only £39, with no income from the fees for marriages, churchings, baptisms and burials, as the curates kept these for themselves. Many of the churches were still unconsecrated and his parishioners were often rude and unco-operative. Haworth and Patrick Brontë gave him the least trouble. The two men had a link in that Mrs Scoresby came from the same district in Ireland as Mr Brontë, and both men shared an interest in natural history. Although Patrick was totally opposed to the Church rates which Scoresby was trying to enforce, he sent a letter of support to him at a meeting in Bradford when he threatened to resign. For his part, Scoresby supported the efforts of Patrick and Arthur to improve education and sanitation in Haworth, and Arthur was to meet with him to discuss these topics on future occasions.

One of the major responsibilities Arthur took over was the supervision and development of the National School. When he came to Haworth it was at a low ebb, with only 60 pupils, and Arthur set about getting more of the children to come to school. He taught religion several times a week and no doubt spent much of his visiting time persuading parents to send their children. He was also responsible for the outlying community of Stanbury and took the lead in getting a schoolroom built there, which could be used as a chapel of ease on Sundays to save local worshippers from having to make the trip to Haworth. He raised £80 from private subscriptions, a very large sum at a time when it exceeded most people's annual income.

Arthur also applied for grants. Fortunately, the interests of social reformers in education was then on the increase and the National Society, which was interested in promoting schools and providing funds, gave a grant of £30. Another grant of £87 came from the Committee of Council, a government body which was the forerunner of the Department of Education. The progressive and forceful Secretary of the Committee was James Kay-Shuttleworth, whom both Arthur and Charlotte were later to meet. Collections raised £10, total expenditure was £214.12s.4½d, and three final donations brought up the total. The last one was for £1.16s.9½d probably put in by Arthur to balance the books. Local tradesmen were employed, the mason being paid £96.12s. 4d, the joiner £55. 3s. 6d; the architect got £6 and the legal fees were £13. 8s.10d. The building, which is still standing, is 35 feet by 20 feet with a height of 12 feet to the wall plate. It was vested in the trusteeship of the Archdeacon of Craven under a deed of conveyance of 5th August, 1848, and was opened for the reception of pupils on 4th September, 1848. This modest building is the only visual reminder of Arthur's stay in Yorkshire.[8]

His early upbringing as a countryman was not forgotten, and for relaxation he used to go walking on the moors. An old man, speaking in 1910 described how as a teenager he had accompanied him: 'He'd a retriever, a girt brown one, it just suited him to see the dog run after t'birds on t'moor game, it would creep within a yard of them.' They used to tickle trout: 'We'd no rods or lines but put our hands under them as they lay under the stones and laiked with them and when we got hold of them we threw them as far as we could into t'field. He wor a verra good hand at it better than me.'[9] Fortunately, at that time and place, the game was not preserved or we could have had the curate in the dock for poaching. His favourite haunt was Smith Bank, near to the Brontë Waterfalls, and, to a young man, the possibility of meeting or seeing the girls from the Parsonage could have been an added attraction.

It was during the autumn of this year, 1845, that Charlotte accidentally found and read Emily's poetry, left open on her writing desk.[10] As she read through the note book she realised the power and depth of her sister's work, urgent and compelling, not the kind of poetry usually written by women. She knew it should be published. Emily was angry at this invasion of her privacy and it took Charlotte time and effort to persuade her to agree to publication. This was just the tonic Charlotte needed to recover from the despair and lethargy she was still feeling following her one-sided love for M. Heger, her Brussels mentor. Then Anne produced some of her poems, very different from Emily's, with, as Charlotte commented, 'A sweet sincere pathos of their own.'[11] Charlotte herself brought out some of her manuscripts and together the three girls spent many an hour in the parlour, when the rest of the household were in bed, revising, copying and planning how to present their work. They kept all this from Mr Brontë for their brother Branwell was causing great difficulty with his drug-taking and drunkenness.

Anne and Emily refused to publish under their own names, indeed, Charlotte herself thought that women writers were often looked upon with condescension, and therefore a pseudonym was needed. They tried to pick names that, while keeping their own initials, were neither overtly masculine nor feminine. Charlotte wrote later, in her preface to the novels of Anne and Emily: 'We veiled our own names under those of Currer, Ellis and Acton Bell; the ambiguous choice being dictated by a sort of conscientious scruple at assuming names positively masculine, while we did not like to declare ourselves women because – without at that time suspecting that our mode of writing and thinking was not what is called "feminine" – we had a vague impression that authoresses are liable to be looked on with prejudice; we noticed how critics sometimes used for their chastisement the weapon of personality, and for their reward a flattery which is not true praise.'[12]

The surname Bell could have been chosen for several reasons as well as the fact that it began with their own initial. All the girls had been baptised in the Bell Chapel at Thornton, Haworth was in the process of raising funds for a new peal of bells in the Church and Bell was, of course, Arthur Nicholls' middle name. Whatever the true reason, Arthur must have felt flattered when he eventually found out what they had done, and Charlotte could not have imagined that one day she would legally bear that same name.

1846-1849

The year 1846 found Patrick Brontë almost totally blind, Charlotte, Emily and Anne trying to decide which of their poems would be included in their first book, Branwell lost further than ever in drink and drugs, and the Rev. Arthur Nicholls quietly and competently taking over nearly all the parish duties. This meant many and frequent visits to the Parsonage, more than would be usual for a curate to make, and they did not go unnoticed by the local population. Rumours spread about the curate and the Parson's daughter but Charlotte had more than enough on her mind at that time to give much thought to innuendo and gossip. The little book of poems had been published, a proper book bound in dark green cloth, able to be bought by the public. The euphoria at the sight of the first copies helped during a difficult time for the family. Martha Brown, the maid, had to go home with a swollen knee; faithful old Tabby the housekeeper had some kind of fit; Branwell was getting worse all the time; Mr Brontë felt he was a burden to everyone; and Charlotte herself was making arrangements for her father's eye operation.

The rumours about Charlotte and Nicholls had even reached Ellen Nussey, Charlotte's close friend since their schooldays and lifelong correspondent, at her home near Birstall. She had been asked if they were true, and wrote to Charlotte who replied in high dudgeon, 'Who gravely asked you whether Miss Brontë was not going to be married to her papa's curate? I scarcely need say that never was rumour more unfounded – it puzzles me to think how it could possibly have originated – a cold far-away sort of civility are the only terms on which I have ever been with Mr Nicholls – I could by no means think of mentioning such a rumour to him even as a joke – it would make me the laughing stock of himself and his fellow curates for half a year to come – they regard me as an old maid, and I regard them, one and all, as highly uninteresting, narrow and unattractive specimens of the "coarser sex".[1] That, as far as Charlotte was concerned, was the end of that. Could it be that the rumours were connecting the right curate with the wrong woman?

About a fortnight later Arthur was even further in Charlotte's bad books. It was the annual Rush-Bearing week.[2] Mr Brontë had arranged for an old friend, the Rev. Thomas Crowther, to give the Sunday School sermons and stay overnight to attend a performance of an oratorio in the church the following day. It was to be a benefit concert for the well-known Haworth tenor, Thomas Parker, who was to sing with Mrs Sunderland, a performer from the Halifax concerts. Many musicians and singers had been recruited from local choirs to perform the accompaniment. Thomas Parker was a Baptist and Arthur and his High Church friends considered it sacrilege to allow a performance by a Baptist in a consecrated church. To show their disapproval the local Puseyite clergy boycotted the occasion, an action considered petty by the more liberal Evangelicals. In any event the church was crowded and Rev. Patrick Brontë made a point of sitting in full view of all with his friends.

The next day Patrick was still well enough to hear the summer examinations of the National School pupils in Haworth, but a week later he was unable to attend the Sunday School anniversary celebrations at Newsholme near Oakworth to which he had been invited. Arthur stepped in and went with Joseph Grant, of Oxenhope, William Busfield, the Rector of Keighley, and Philip Eggleston, then Curate of Ingrow cum Hainworth, to perform the necessary duties. Patrick Brontë's sight had now become so bad that, until some treatment had been carried out, Arthur would have to take over completely. Charlotte and Emily decided to go to Manchester to see if they could find a suitable surgeon. At the Manchester Institution for Curing the Diseases of the Eye they described their father's symptoms to Dr William James Wilson, M.R.C.S., who was one of the leading eye specialists of his time. He was also on the staff of the Manchester Infirmary, well-known and respected. He could not tell from the girls' description whether the eyes were ready for an operation and needed to see Patrick Brontë himself. They were to return with him and, if it proved right, the operation would be carried out. Many arrangements of a domestic and parochial kind had to be made as in those days the operation required a long convalescence and Patrick would be away for at least a month. Charlotte was to accompany him, leaving Emily and Anne in charge at home and Arthur in charge of the parish business. During the five weeks Mr Brontë was recuperating

Arthur conducted 20 baptisms and 17 burials, as well as the usual Sunday Services and duties at the Schools, both in Haworth and Stanbury. His Ordination as a priest was due to take place in Ripon Cathedral on 20th September. Patrick and Charlotte were not due back until later that week so Arthur arranged for Joseph Grant to cover his Sunday duties. This important event in his life was not mentioned in Charlotte's frequent letters to Ellen and seems to have passed by quite unnoticed, perhaps due to the worry of her father's operation. Ten deacons and twenty priests were ordained that day by the Rt. Reverend Charles Thomas Longley, Lord Bishop of Ripon. It must have been a proud and moving moment for Arthur but sad in that he had no one with whom to share it.

He returned to Haworth and continued his duties as conscientiously as ever, while Patrick's eyesight continued to improve. Although he had had only the cataract from his left eye removed, he could now begin to be more independent, and by November Arthur felt able to ask for a three-week holiday in order to visit his Irish relatives. Mr Brontë eased himself gradually back to his duties, first by just reading the prayers in church and then by taking services. Charlotte wrote to Ellen on November 17: 'Papa continues to do well – he read prayers in Church twice last Sunday – next Sunday he will have to take the whole duty of the three services as Mr Nicholls is in Ireland'[3] While Arthur was enjoying his well-earned holiday Patrick was not fit enough to manage without some help and Rev. Philip Eggleston came over to help Mr Brontë with his duties, conducting funerals on 8th and 15th November.[4]

Philip had been licensed on 16th October by the Rector of Keighley, acting for the Bishop of Ripon, to be Curate and incumbent of the new church of St Paul's at Denholme Gate. The new Church was to be consecrated on 20th November by the Bishop, Dr Longley, and, although Philip would have been in the midst of the arrangements, he found time to come over and conduct the funerals. The consecration was a lavish ceremony led by the Bishop of Ripon with the Rev. Dr Scoresby of Bradford preaching the sermon, followed by luncheon for nearly 200 people.[5] It seems to have been attended by all the local clergy, including: Charnock, Sowden, Grant, Crowther and Busfield. Both Arthur, away in Ireland, and Patrick, recuperating, would have been sorry to have missed the ceremony.

The end of 1846 was not a very happy time for the Brontë family: Branwell had a visit from a Sheriff's Officer from York with a demand to pay his debts; the weather that winter was extraordinarily bad with bitter winds and biting frost; Anne had asthma very badly and Emily a very bad cold. Charlotte complained to Ellen that she could not keep warm! Mr Brontë, only recently recovered from his operation, caught influenza, and the running of the parish was once more left to Arthur.

The inhabitants of rural areas have always been slow to accept newcomers, and Haworth was no exception, but Rev. Arthur Nicholls was becoming a more familiar figure as he went about the village visiting the sick, conducting services in the church, or just taking the outdoor exercise he enjoyed so much. He made frequent visits to the Parsonage to consult with Mr Brontë and to the school to teach religious education. Charlotte was immersed in writing *Jane Eyre*, which she had begun in Manchester, and had hardly any interest in anything else, much less the doings of a humble curate.

With the coming of spring and better weather Mr Brontë recovered some of his old vigour. Branwell was going through a quieter period and Charlotte felt able to invite Ellen Nussey to visit her at Haworth. She was worried that Arthur would be leaving soon – he had been there two years and would now be looking for preferment. She asked Ellen on June 29th: 'When can you come to Haworth? Another period of fine weather is passing without you – I fear your visit will be dull indeed – for it is doubtful whether there will even be a curate here to enliven you – Mr Nicholls is likely to get a district ere long and papa will be left without assistance, for how long I do not know – this rather troubles me – the whole duty is too much for him at his age – he is pretty well but often complains of weakness.'[6]

Later in the year, Ellen's praise of Arthur in her letters to Charlotte earned her the brusque reply: 'I cannot for my life see those interesting germs of goodness in him you discovered. His narrowness of mind always strikes me chiefly – I fear he is indebted to your imagination for his hidden treasures.'[7] Although Charlotte found nothing to like in Arthur, she realised her father would be lost without him, and perhaps began to take more notice of the role he played in the smooth running of the parish. Arthur seemed to have dropped his intention of moving on; perhaps he was beginning to take a greater interest in Charlotte.

It could hardly be his relationship with his flock as he was now engaged in a long-running battle with the women of Haworth. For many years it had been the custom for washing to be spread out to dry on the tombstones in the churchyard but Arthur saw this as an affront both to the dignity of the church and lack of respect for the dead. He began a fierce campaign to have it stopped. He set out for Ireland for a three-week holiday in September, leaving behind so much bad feeling that: 'Many of the parishioners express a desire that he should not recross the Channel but remain quietly where he is – not the feeling that should exist between shepherd and flock.' But he came back nothing daunted and carried on the fight with vigour. At last he got his way and the washerwomen had to make other arrangements. Even the Brontë washing had to be dried elsewhere – in John Brown's field at a charge of two shillings per year. Mr Brontë watched the episode with some amusement. At the end of the controversy he wrote a verse entitled *Church Reform* to commemorate the event and Arthur kept a copy of it all his life.[8]

In the same year Arthur found another new interest – the Haworth Mechanics' Institute. There was an Institute in Keighley, but attending meetings there necessitated a round walk of seven or eight miles which made for a long evening. The Haworth Institute was formed in 1845 as an answer to this difficulty, and among the first members were the clergymen, Brontë, Nicholls and Grant.[9] It was run by a committee of 12 members and a secretary appointed by vote. A small library was built up and public lectures were held to which members were admitted free while visitors paid 3d each. Both men and women could join and Charlotte was a life member. Meetings were held in a room in Newell Hill, just off Main Street. Arthur was an active member and two years later was appointed President. By 1851 the membership was over 100.

On October 16th *Jane Eyre* was published by Smith Elder, & Co. of Cornhill, soon afterwards followed by *Wuthering Heights* and *Agnes Grey,* published together in three volumes by Thomas Newby. *Jane Eyre* was an instant success and the first edition had sold out in three months. Whilst not so successful, her two sisters had reason to hope, and for the girls, if not for poor Branwell, who was rapidly going downhill, 1847 ended on a note of optimism.

Jane Eyre had taken the public by storm and had excited

much interest in the reviews and speculation about the identity of Currer Bell. Charlotte really had to say something to her father, but told no one else. He was pleased and proud, and it helped to take his mind off the troubles they were having with Branwell. Arthur could only watch from the sidelines as the young man gradually declined into self-pity and ill health. It was fortunate that Arthur had come to Haworth before the younger members of the Brontë family had died, as it gave him insight into the family which would prove a common bond between himself and Charlotte as time went on. He had known Branwell before he was so ill, was aware of his father's disappointment and care for him, his sisters' exasperation and impatience with his drink and drug habits. He knew of Emily's love of animals, Anne's asthma and Charlotte's courage, but he knew nothing of their writing, although rumours were beginning to spread. Charlotte had occasion to write to Ellen Nussey, who was guessing at the truth, that she gave no one the right to hint or affirm that she was publishing.[10]

In June, Anne's novel, *The Tenant of Wildfell Hall,* was published, and in July Charlotte and Anne left Emily and their father to take charge of the increasingly disturbed Branwell while they visited their publishers in London. By the end of that month Charlotte wrote to Ellen that, 'Branwell is in the same conduct as ever – papa, sometimes all of us, have sad nights with him.'[11]

In early September, Arthur Nicholls had been invited to Denholme Gate to perform the happy duty of baptising Ada, the first child of Philip Eggleston and his wife, Elizabeth. The story of their marriage is a tragedy worthy of the Brontës themselves. They had four children who all died young, the eldest reaching just 4 years 7 months. Elizabeth herself died in 1857 aged only 27, and four years later Philip joined his family in the grave at the age of 47.[12]

By now Branwell was in a bad way. He had a hacking cough and was so thin his clothes hung off him. He died at 9 o'clock on Sunday morning, September 24th, 1848, with the family round him. He was only 31 years of age. In spite of the disappointment and trouble he had caused, Charlotte wrote, 'My poor father naturally thought more of his only son than of his daughters and, much and long as he had suffered on his account, he cried out in his loss like David for that of Absalom – my son! my son! and refused to be comforted.'[13]

A few days later, Charlotte herself was forced to take to her bed with bilious fever and a headache. Branwell's burial on September 28th was conducted by Patrick Brontë's old friend, William Morgan. His body was interred in the family vault under the church. It was the custom in Haworth to preach a funeral sermon on the first Sunday after a burial and Patrick asked Arthur to perform this sad duty. Arthur was assisted by Joseph Grant of Oxenhope, a friend of Arthur's and helpful to him on many occasions. He was Patrick's curate, responsible for Oxenhope, and became the incumbent there when the new church was consecrated on 11th October, 1849. [14]

On the day of the service it was unseasonably cold. There was a bitter wind blowing and the church was damp and draughty. Emily, already suffering a cold and a cough, caught a chill. By the middle of October it was apparent that she was very ill and her condition worsened throughout November. She continued to perform her normal household tasks and declared, when the family suggested medical help, that 'no poisoning doctor should come near her'. By the middle of December it was clear that she was close to death, but she still would not stay in bed. She died on 19th December, 1848, just three months after Branwell. Again Arthur had a sad duty to perform for the family he was getting to know so much better. On 22nd December he met the funeral party at the south door of the church, Mr Brontë leading, accompanied by Emily's dog, Keeper, and followed by Charlotte and Anne, who was herself looking very frail. Behind came the old servant, Tabby, and the young servant, Martha Brown. For the second time that year the vault was opened to receive a member of the family.

The new year, 1849, was stormy and cold, and Haworth was in the grip of an epidemic of influenza. Both Patrick and Anne were confined to bed and Arthur was performing most of the duties once again. It was obvious that Anne was not recovering and Mr Brontë decided they needed a second opinion. Mr Teale, a well-known Leeds specialist in consumption, came to the Parsonage and examined her with a stethoscope.[15] His diagnosis was consumption of both lungs, which had progressed too far to cure and he told the family frankly that Anne had not long to live. Dr Wheeler undertook her treatment which included blisters, pills, cod-liver oil and carbonate of iron. Unlike Emily, she was willing to try anything to get well. Of course, none of these helped and she was slowly but inexorably failing before the eyes of Charlotte and all who knew her. She was obsessed with the idea that if she could get to the seaside she might improve, but the weather was dreadful. There was no question of going until the spring.

In February Anne had a slight remission and Charlotte had time to make a fair copy of the first volume of her new novel, *Shirley*, but, by mid-March, Anne's symptoms were just as bad again and she was hankering after a trip to Scarborough. Charlotte was not happy about Anne travelling in her present state but she knew this might be one of her last wishes. After consulting Mr Teale, who raised no objections, she set about making the arrangements. Charlotte and Ellen were to accompany Anne. That meant that Mr Brontë would be on his own at the Parsonage, except, of course, for the servants, and Charlotte tried to make provision for Arthur to keep her father company. However, as she wrote to Ellen on May 16: 'You ask what I have arranged about leaving Papa. I could make no special arrangement. He wishes me to go with Anne and will not hear of Mr Nicholls coming or anything of that kind.'[16] The only way Arthur was allowed to help was to take the Parsonage dogs for their daily walk, but at least this gave him the opportunity to keep an eye on the old man.

On Thursday, 24 May, about mid-day, Martha Brown, Nicholls, Ellen and Charlotte helped Anne into the carriage that was to take the little party to Keighley Station. Patrick Brontë, Arthur, lame old Tabby, and Martha with the dogs, Keeper and Flossie, stood at the gate to watch their departure. Keeper stood stock still but Flossie made off after the carriage. Arthur ran after her and caught her outside his lodgings at Sexton House and held her tightly until the carriage was round the corner. In later years Martha said that death was written clearly on Anne's face. How right she was. Four days later in the lodging house at No. 2 The Cliff, Scarborough, Anne died. She was buried on 30th May, 1849, in St Mary's churchyard, Scarborough, to save Mr Brontë the distress of opening the family vault for the third time in nine months.

Mr Brontë wrote and told Charlotte not to come home immediately but to remain at the seaside for a while to recover from her distress and to build up her strength. She and Ellen stayed a few more days at Scarborough, moved to Filey for a week, then to Easton near Bridlington, where she continued her work on *Shirley*. The return home could not be put off for ever and on 20th June Ellen and Charlotte returned to their respective families.

1849-1852

It was a moment Charlotte was dreading. When she arrived home she found the Parsonage clean and bright and the servants and her father well. The dogs were delighted to see her and eagerly sniffed around as if expecting Anne and Emily to come. She tried to feel glad to be back but the emptiness and the silence made her sad. The only cure for her loneliness was in her writing, and she flung herself into finishing *Shirley*.

Arthur also had known personal sadness that year, his father, William Nichols *(sic)*, had died over in Ireland, at the age of 80, leaving William and George, Arthur's two oldest brothers, to run the family farm at Tully.

Mr Brontë too needed something more than his pastoral work to help him at this time and he took up a cause dear to his heart – the health of the people of Haworth. He had for a long time worried about the poor sanitation and impure water supply which he believed caused such a high death rate in the village, and he and Arthur organised a petition to be sent to the General Board of Health in London which had recently been set up in response to the scare of a second cholera epidemic (1848). It was dated 28th August, 1849, and signed by P. Brontë, A.B., incumbent, A. B. Nicholls, A.B., curate, E. S. Hall, surgeon, John B. Wheelhouse, Surgeon, and by many of the people of Haworth. While they waited a reply, life went on as usual. Patrick, suffering from bronchitis, had arranged for William Morgan to go to the Consistory Court in York and take out Letters of Administration on his behalf to enable him (Patrick) to deal with Anne's estate.[1] Mr. Morgan visited Haworth on 3rd September as he required the signature of Patrick, and those of Arthur and William Summerscale, the National School teacher, in order to carry out his commission. A few days later another caller at the house was James Taylor, of Smith Elder & Co. He was on his way home from Scotland and broke his journey to pick up the now finished manuscript of *Shirley*. Charlotte thought him very peculiar.

Patrick received a reply from the Board of Health saying they could take no action unless the petition was supported by one-tenth of the rate-payers, so he and Arthur set to work again to obtain the extra signatures.[2] Eventually the Board agreed to send an investigator, but it was two years before any remedial work was done by the authorities.

Charlotte went for a week's holiday at Ellen Nussey's home and combined this with a visit to the dentist, on 24th October .[3] Two days later, *Shirley* was published and her years of fame began as people began to recognise themselves in her characters and guessed her identity. In November she went to stay with George Smith's mother in London, and met some of the literary lions of the day. She returned home to the knowledge that *Jane Eyre* had been read all over the district and *Shirley* was now in demand.

In January, 1850, Ellen wrote to tell Charlotte about the notoriety of *Shirley* and, on the 19th of that month, Charlotte replied, 'All that you tell me about the notoriety of *Shirley* in Dewsbury is as good as an emetic to me. I should really "go off at side" if I thought too much about it. Mr Nicholls having finished *Jane Eyre* is now crying out for the other book – he is to have it next week – much good may it do him.'[4] In the event it did both Arthur and Charlotte a lot of good. She discovered that, under his deep reserve, he had a sense of humour. His reaction when reading the description of the curates in his room at Sexton House was such that his landlady thought he had had a brainstorm. He laughed uproariously, clapped his hands and stamped on the floor. It showed Charlotte in a different light – not just as a middle-aged spinster but as a woman with sharp powers of observation and a clever mind. Arthur read the passages about the curates to Patrick and together they enjoyed them. Quietly and unobtrusively Charlotte and Arthur were becoming closer. At this time, Arthur was President of Haworth Mechanics' Institute. A meeting was called of all members to discuss the ordering *of Jane Eyre* and *Shirley* for their small library. All the members wanted to borrow them so they had to cast lots: whoever got the volume was allowed to keep it two days and was fined one shilling a day if they retained it longer. Arthur was said to have presented Charlotte with a Book of Common Prayer to commemorate the publication of *Shirley* and by March a few curious tourists were making their way to Haworth. Sir James and Lady Kay-Shuttleworth of Gawthorpe Hall, Burnley, were great admirers of Charlotte's work and arrived at the Parsonage to persuade her to visit them.[5] She was reluctant to go, but the invitation was made in the presence of her father, who practically accepted for her. She went next day and stayed for three weeks. She was glad she had been and felt better for it.

Whilst Charlotte was busy with her own affairs, Patrick Brontë and Arthur had to attend to parish matters. In April, Benjamin Herschel Babbage, the inspector from the General Board of Health, arrived and started his enquiries. He was horrified at what he found. There were no sewers, no water closets, an average of one privy for every four-and-a-half houses, but in Gauger's Croft one privy to 24 houses. Some were in the public streets and exposed to the passers-by. Cesspits were overflowing down Main Street next to a communal water supply. There were only two wells and nine pumps. The water was contaminated and, often, even the animals would not drink it; it was draining through the churchyard into wells and pumps. The enquiry lasted three days and had to be moved from the vestry to the National Schoolroom as so many people attended. In spite of the damning report which resulted, it was to be many years before real improvements were effected.

Also in April, Arthur drew Mr Brontë's attention to the fact that people were using the path across church lands to reach the mill without paying for the privilege of its use, which could with time give them an inalienable right of way. They wrote to the Trustees to try to clear the matter up and to see if anything could be done without recourse to law, combining the letter with a request for the Trustees to inspect the Parsonage as the roof was in a bad state. Work was quickly put in hand to mend the roof but nothing further seems to have been recorded about the problem over the right of way.

While the repairs to the Parsonage were under way, Charlotte went off to London, leaving Martha Redman, daughter of the Parish Clerk, and the two servants in charge. She stayed away until the middle of July, obviously enjoying her independence and leaving her father to manage without her, despite all the upset the work caused.

Scarcely a month after returning home, Charlotte was off on her travels again – this time to stay with the Kay-Shuttleworths in the Lake District. It was here she met Mrs Gaskell, and the two women became close friends, exchanging confidences and, after the visit was over, letters. Charlotte was very lonely on returning home and spent much time reading books and newspapers. She read about the Pope, who had appointed Nicholas Wiseman as Cardinal and Archbishop of Westminster. Roman Catholic Bishoprics in England had not been known since the time of Elizabeth I. Nicholas Wiseman, well-known for persuading Puseyites to turn to Rome, was hated by the Anglicans. Some even thought he was looking to become Pope himself and that if this happened he would abolish the celibacy of priests. This would remove a big obstacle in the way of reunion with the Church of England. Patrick Brontë took up his pen and wrote to the *Leeds Intelligencer*, saying the Catholics and Dissenters should be warned that, if they overthrew the Church of England, all religion would be overthrown. The issue also touched Arthur, who might have been considered sympathetic being on the Puseyite wing of the Church, but, no, he too was vehemently against it. He went to a meeting of clergymen in Leeds on 27th November, where a resolution was passed condemning the Pope for ignoring the existence of the Church of England, dishonouring the Queen, and sowing the seeds of strife throughout the land. This was signed by 250 clergymen, including Arthur himself. No doubt the whole furore would have been a regular topic of discussion between Arthur, Patrick and Charlotte, who was strongly anti-Catholic and took a keen interest in Church politics.

After this diversion Charlotte was once more affected with wanderlust. She went to stay with Harriet Martineau and then on to visit Ellen, with whom she stayed over Christmas, leaving her father in the lonely Parsonage yet again when her presence would have been of great comfort to him. There had been more rumours, passed on by Ellen, that Charlotte was to marry, and again Charlotte was at pains to let Ellen know they were entirely groundless: 'I wish, dear Ellen, you would tell me what is this "Twaddle about my marrying etc.", which you hear. If I knew the details I would have a better chance of guessing the quarter from which such gossip comes; as it is I am quite at a loss. I think I have scarcely seen a single man with whom such union would be possible since I left London. Doubtless there are men whom, if I chose to encourage, I might marry, but no matrimonial lot is even offered me which seems to me truly desirable, and, even if that were not the case, there would be many obstacles. The least allusion to such a thing is most offensive to Papa.'[6]

Patrick had obviously been worried that Charlotte had met

someone in London, and Ellen thought she had George Smith in mind. At the beginning of 1851 she wrote to Ellen about Smith: 'I am content to have him as a friend and pray God to continue to me the common sense to look on one so young, so rising and so hopeful in no other light.' To take her mind off any romantic notions, Patrick urged her to start another book. In April, James Taylor, a partner in Smith and Elder, again visited Haworth; this time he proposed to her. Charlotte could not stand the sight of him – he reminded her too much of Branwell – and refused his offer. Strangely enough, her father approved of Taylor and gave Charlotte the impression that he would have made no objection.

The day Taylor left, Patrick became ill and had to take to his bed, leaving Arthur once more in charge. The house was quiet, Charlotte was lonely and Arthur was the only person she saw apart from the servants. She was 35 that year and felt ugly and middle-aged. Another trip to London was arranged, which her father worried about. 'Tabby, Martha and Papa – all these fancy I am somehow – by some mysterious process to be married in London – or to engage myself to matrimony. How I smile internally! How groundless and impossible is the idea! Papa seriously told me that if I married and left him – he should give up housekeeping and go into lodgings!!'[7] Undeterred by her father's objections, Charlotte set off with some new clothes and a pink-lined bonnet, leaving him to supervise the redecoration of the downstairs rooms and Arthur to step into the breach in the event of Patrick becoming ill. It was during this visit that George Smith persuaded Charlotte to sit for George Richmond to paint her portrait. She was not allowed to see it until it was finished and when she was shown it she burst into tears – it reminded her so of her sisters. Smith had the portrait and a smaller one of the Duke of Wellington sent to the Parsonage, where they arrived on August 1st and were hung in the dining room.

Arthur Nicholls' work-load was increasingly heavier. His efforts for the National School were bearing fruit – the numbers had increased dramatically, from 60 when he arrived to over 200. One old lady, a friend of Tabitha Brown, recalling her childhood, remembered his going into school twice a week accompanied by his brown retriever, and bringing sweets for the children. Others had not so happy memories of the results of his belief in fresh air. William Wood recalled seeing him walking to the field behind the Parsonage every morning after breakfast where he rushed up and down swinging his arms vigorously. If it was frosty he beat his arms across his chest and stamped his feet. When he had kept this up for about half an hour and had 'got himself into a glow' he'd come tearing down the street and into the school-room throwing open every window to let in 'real live air'. In winter there was only one small stove to heat the school and the children were almost blue with cold.[8] Arthur was recalled as being strict but fair: there was no horseplay when he was in charge.

Church attendance had also substantially increased. As well as his duties at Haworth, he now supervised the school and the small church which he had had built at Stanbury and which had opened in September, 1848. His fellow curate, James Grant, largely ascribed the success of the school and the increasing congregation there to Arthur's efforts. He visited the sick, particularly those in the more distant parts of the parish that Mr Brontë now had difficulty in reaching, and his Saturday mornings were still taken up by private tutoring in order to increase his income. Patrick knew he would never be able to cope without him, even more so now he was not as strong as formerly, and he was worried that the grant from the Church Pastoral Aid Society which had enabled him to pay Arthur's salary would not be renewed for the coming year. He was relieved when, after two months' delay, the grant was allowed, but he immediately applied for a further grant to employ a lay reader to help Arthur, acknowledging his hard work and dedication.

While Charlotte was away she wrote to Patrick, 'Hoping you are well, dear Papa, and with kind regards to Mr Nicholls, Tabby and Martha, also poor old Keeper and Flossie. I am glad the Parlour is done now and you have got safely settled . . .'[9] It was the first time she had mentioned Arthur with kindness in that manner. Perhaps she was beginning to realise his true character at last. Arthur was due to take his month's annual holiday at the end of July, as usual visiting his Irish relatives. The evening before he was due to begin his journey, he invited himself to tea at the Parsonage, and Charlotte described his behaviour to Ellen as, 'somewhat peculiarly for him – being extremely good – mild and uncontentious'. He set off in high spirits for his trip, leaving Charlotte hoping that her father would be able to manage on his own. She had begun to write *Villette* and was now trying to make more progress. Life in Haworth was quiet and her father had no major problems but she found it difficult to settle to her work. It was with a note of relief that she wrote, 'Papa, it cheers me to say

– has continued pretty well all that time of Mr Nicholl's absence – he is now expected back next Sunday.' For once it seems she would be pleased to see him.

In October, after Arthur's return, while Charlotte was still feeling depressed and unsettled, Tabby caught influenza, Martha also succumbed and suffered two attacks of quinsy, and Patrick caught a cold. Charlotte had her hands full nursing them all and at the beginning of November herself fell ill. In her nervous and run-down condition she immediately believed she had fallen victim to the tuberculosis that had killed her sisters but, when the doctor was consulted, it was found to be severe inflammation of the liver. She did not really believe him and did not improve. The doctor prescribed more medicine including the infamous 'blue pill': mercury was one of its ingredients and, before long, she was exhibiting the classic symptoms of mercury poisoning – mouth ulcers, loose teeth and over-salivation. She stopped taking the pills and was then given other medicine to counteract the effect. It was not until the end of January that she was able to visit Ellen to complete her recuperation. On her return she set to work and by 29th March had completed the draft of her first volume of *Villette*. She discouraged visitors, declined invitations, and carried out just those domestic duties that could not be avoided, only to find again that she could not settle to her writing. Eventually she decided to take a short break on her own to visit Anne's grave at Scarborough and spend some time at Filey. The doctor thought this a good idea and consequently she set out at the end of May to stay at Cliff House.

On June 2nd, 1852, in a letter to her father she wrote, 'On Sunday afternoon I went to a church which I should like Mr Nicholls to see. It was certainly not more than thrice the length and breadth of our passage – floored with brick – the walls green with mould – the pews painted white but the paint almost all worn off with time and decay – at one end there is a little gallery for the singers – and when these personages stood up to perform – they all turned their backs upon the congregation – and the congregation turned their backs on the pulpit and parson. The effect of this manoeuvre was so ludicrous – I could hardly help laughing – had Mr Nicholls been here – he certainly would have laughed out. Looking up at the gallery and seeing only the broad backs of the singers presented to their audience was excessively grotesque.'[10] The holiday did her good and she returned to Haworth much improved both physically and mentally.

It was lucky she did. Only a fortnight after her return Patrick suffered a minor stroke. The burden of nursing fell once more on her and the burden of the parish on Arthur. Inevitably they were thrown together in their joint effort to assist. For all of August and most of September the parish was in Arthur's capable hands, while Charlotte was trying to write *Villette* as she nursed her father. They had a chance to observe each other's behaviour in difficult circumstances and it is significant that there were no sarcastic references to Arthur in any of Charlotte's letters to Ellen. Gradually, as the old man improved, Charlotte could devote more time to her work. On 20th November she at last sent *Villette* off to Cornhill and went to visit Ellen for a few days.

- 5 -
Proposal and Rejection

After her return home, not having become engaged, as rumour said she might, Arthur decided he was now free to speak of his feelings towards her. On 13th December he proposed. Charlotte told Ellen afterwards that she had long suspected how he felt and had noticed his attitude towards her and the significant glances he had given her.

Arthur had been in love with her for months. He really had a severe case of love-sickness which was manifesting itself physically. He had become low-spirited and sickly and thought seriously of returning to Ireland. On Monday he went to the Parsonage for his normal weekly tea and talk with Mr Brontë on parish and school matters. He was tired of the sarcastic remarks Patrick kept making regarding his depressed and nervous state and was determined also to speak to him about his personal feelings. It was now or never. After tea in Mr Brontë's study, Charlotte withdrew to the dining room as was her custom. Arthur was so nervous his manner became stilted and unnatural. He found he dare not speak to Charlotte's father to ask permission to marry her, and until between eight and nine o'clock they spoke only of normal mundane business. When he could stand it no longer Arthur took his leave of the old man, but, instead of going out of the door, his courage returned and he went into the dining room. He saw Charlotte sitting there, and, deathly pale, trembling with nervousness and speaking in a low voice, asked her to marry him. She was shocked, not so much by the proposal, but by the state he was in. She was used to seeing him always so controlled and 'statue-like'. Suddenly she realised there was more to the curate than she had ever imagined. He asked her to give him some hope and she asked if he had spoken to her father. When he confessed that he had not had the courage to do so, she replied, in accordance with the social mores of the time, that she would give him his answer the following day and asked him to leave. By now he was so overcome he could hardly move and she had to half lead and half push him out of the room to return to his lodgings. Charlotte decided to take matters into her own hands and, immediately she heard the slam of the front door, she went in to see her father.

She told him that Arthur wished to marry her and had proposed. Mr Brontë was furious, with anger quite disproportionate to the circumstances, calling Arthur terrible names and saying dreadful things about him. Charlotte poured out her feelings to Ellen: 'If I had loved Mr N. and had heard such epithets applied as were used – it would have transported me past my patience – as it was – my blood boiled with a sense of injustice.'[1] He worked himself up to such a pitch that his eyes became bloodshot and the veins on his neck stood out. Charlotte, afraid of inducing another stroke, said that the next day she would write to Arthur refusing him. She was not in love with him, but her keen sense of justice made her pity him deeply for the harsh treatment given him by her father. He had not deserved that.

The Parsonage was not a large enough house for the servants not to have heard the furore and before long the whole village had heard about it. Tabby thought it was a terrible business, Martha was bitter about Arthur, and John Brown said he would like to shoot him. Arthur's landlady, Mrs Brown, was upset because, since he came in on that Monday evening, he had shut himself in his room and refused all his meals. On the following Monday Mr Brontë sent a very cruel note to Arthur in which he demanded his resignation, writing to him with hardness and contempt. He showed it to Charlotte before sending it and she was so shocked by its virulence that she added a note of her own to say, that, although she could never reciprocate Arthur's feeling, she had no wish to be in any way associated with 'sentiments calculated to give him pain' and encouraged him to keep up his spirits and courage.

Arthur in turn offered to resign. Ironically, the drama and the injustice of the episode was just the thing to arouse Charlotte's interest in Nicholls – she had always supported the underdog – and Mr Brontë was succeeding in strengthening the very feelings he was fulminating against. That Sunday Arthur arranged for a substitute to take the services in church and remained locked in his room. Perhaps Charlotte's few words at the end of her father's letter gave him some hope because he wrote to Mr Brontë and asked to withdraw his resignation. Patrick would not entertain this unless Arthur gave his written promise 'never to broach the obnoxious subject' again, either to him, or to Charlotte.[2] It was a promise he could neither give nor keep.

The two men had not yet met each other face to face since that Monday evening and the villagers were now taking sides; mostly they were supporting Mr Brontë, and, now Miss Brontë was a celebrity, probably thought she should marry someone more important than a curate. Charlotte felt she understood Arthur better now and wrote further to Ellen: 'They don't understand the nature of his (Arthur's) feelings, but I now see what they are. Mr N. is one of those who attach themselves to very few, whose sensations are close and deep, like an underground stream, running strong but in a narrow channel. He continues restless and ill, he carefully performs the occasional duty, but does not come near the church, procuring a substitute every Sunday.'[3] Since there had been no promise from Arthur, the matter of his resignation was unsettled and Charlotte felt he would probably go to Australia. Without loving him, she did not like to think of him suffering in solitude and wished him to be somewhere else where he could be happier.

Charlotte made sure that she was elsewhere. Using the excuse that she had to see her publishers, she left for London on 5th January, 1853, wishing that, 'Papa would resume his tranquillity and Mr Nicholls his beef and pudding.'[4]

In the meantime, Arthur had sent to the United Society for the Propagation of the Gospel for an application form to take up missionary work overseas. He filled it in and returned it on 28th January , the very day of the publication of *Villette*.[5]

In reply to the question on the form, 'What considerations have led you to offer yourself for missionary employment?', he stated, 'I have for some time felt a strong inclination to assist in ministering to the thousands of our fellow countrymen who by emigration have been in great measure deprived of the means of grace.' He added in his covering letter that he wished to offer himself as a candidate for employment in the Australian Colonies and that his present engagement would end by the end of May. Perhaps he chose Australia because one of his sisters, Jane, had emigrated there.

He gave as his referees, Patrick Brontë, Dr Burnett, Vicar of Bradford, his friends Sutcliffe Sowden of Hebden Bridge and Joseph Grant from Oxenhope, and Rev. William Cartman, the schoolmaster from Skipton. Mr Brontë's reference was written in his usual economic style but in the circumstances rather tongue in cheek. He stated that during the seven years of his curacy at Haworth Arthur had behaved himself, 'wisely, soberly and piously'. Also mentioned were his good work for the Sunday School, his freedom from pecuniary embarrassments, his wary and prudent character and his sound and orthodox principles . It was clear that he wanted to make sure that Arthur went and the further away the better. He could hardly have said they were not on speaking terms because he had had the temerity to propose to his daughter, nor that he thought Arthur 'a damned Puseyite', but he was not beyond dissembling when it came to getting his own way.

Arthur's other references were all glowing. Joseph Grant and Sutcliffe Sowden, both of whom had known him as a friend as well as a colleague for eight years, mentioned his 'piety and zeal', his good work for the school and his prudent habits. Sowden also revealed that he was 'somewhat troubled by Rheumatism' but expected it would leave him when spring arrived. William Cartman wrote a very fulsome reply in which he stated that 'Mr Brontë has often detailed to me his valuable services and has frequently said that, sh'd he leave him, he should not know how to supply his place.' Like Mr Brontë, Dr Burnett, the Vicar of Bradford, gave a short reply, including the observation that 'he has conducted himself with great prudence and distinction among a rude, dissenting population and by his exertions the Church has gained great ground'.

While Charlotte was enjoying her month in London and the publication of *Villette*, she received two letters from her father, both showing that his feelings towards Arthur had not changed. On 19th January, 1853, he wrote, 'You may wish to know how we have been getting on here especially in respect to <u>master</u> and <u>man</u>. On yesterday I preached twice, but my man was every way very queer – He shunned me , as if I had been a Cobra de Capello – turning his head from the quarter where I was and hustling away amongst the crowd, to avoid contact – his countenance was strongly indicative of mortified pride, and malevolent resentment.' He went on to say people were noticing his strange behaviour and speculating as to its cause and further, 'You thought me too severe – but I was not candid enough – this conduct might have been excus'd by the world in a confirmed rake – or unprincipled Army Officer, but in a clergyman it is justly chargeable with base design and inconsistency. I earnestly wish that he had another and better situation – as I can never trust him any more in things of importance – I wish him no ill – but rather good, and wish that every woman may avoid him for ever, unless she should be determined on her own misery – all the produce of the Australian diggins [referring to the gold rush] would not make him and any wife he might have happy . . .'⁶ One hesitates to think what Mr Brontë's reaction would have been had the proposal to Charlotte come from a 'confirmed rake'. Arthur's misery, in the face of Charlotte's refusal and Patrick's implacable anger and scorn, was plain to see. Far from his usual calm attitude, he was teetering on the edge of a nervous breakdown.

Another letter, written in the name of Flossy, perhaps in an attempt to be amusing, was mean and sarcastic, especially as Arthur had been the only one to take the Parsonage dogs out for their run in all weathers. In it Patrick, as Flossy, wrote, 'I see people cheating one another, and appearing to be friends – many are the disagreeable discoveries which I make, which you would hardly believe if I were to tell them – one thing I have lately seen, which I wish to mention – no one takes me out to walk now, the weather is too cold or wet for my master to walk in, and my former travelling companion (Arthur) has lost all his apparent kindness, scolds me and looks black upon me . . . Ah! my dear mistress, trust dogs rather than men – they are very selfish . . .'⁷ What Charlotte made of this correspondence can only be surmised but it did not help her to forget recent events and probably furthered, rather than hindered, Arthur's cause. Dreading her return home, Charlotte asked Ellen to meet her at Keighley station and to go to Haworth with her for a short while, so that she would not have to face her father alone.

Ellen readily agreed, only too happy to be there at the seat of the action. The reviews of *Villette* came out and these served to take Mr Brontë's mind off Arthur for a little. Things may have become calmer in the Parsonage but, in Sexton House, Arthur was sad and despondent. He and Patrick were still avoiding each other and matters were still unresolved. No reply had come from the U.S.P.G. and Arthur wrote again to them on 23rd February, 'I some time ago addressed an application to the Society for an appointment to the Australian Colonies. As I have had no reply I shall feel obliged by your kindly informing me, whether my letter has been received, and if so, when is it probable that I shall have a definite answer?' They replied by return of post and invited him to London for an interview. On February 26th, only three days after his previous letter Arthur wrote again, `Since the date of my application, owing to the solicitations of friends, some doubts have occurred to me as to the desirableness of leaving the Country at present. When I have fully made up my mind upon the point I will communicate with you.' What had happened in those three days to make him change his mind? His friends may have persuaded him that if he stayed he might yet have a chance of winning over Mr Brontë, whereas in Australia any hope he had ever had was gone, or, perhaps in his distraught state, he was incapable of making his mind up to any firm course of action.

He could not hide away for ever, and the villagers got used to seeing him walking disconsolately around, doing those parochial tasks which could not be avoided. In March, Dr Longley, the Bishop of Ripon, was to visit Haworth, and the curates of Oxenhope and Oakworth as well as Arthur were all invited to tea and supper. Now Patrick and Arthur had to meet, there was no way it could be avoided. Charlotte, as hostess, was anxious that all should go smoothly. Great preparations were made for cleaning and catering and extra help was brought in for Martha in the kitchen. The church was swept and dusted. When Dr Longley arrived he proved to be friendly and perceptive; Charlotte wrote that he was, 'certainly a most charming little Bishop, the most benignant little gentleman that ever put on lawn sleeves'. A fine description for a future Archbishop of York and later of Canterbury!

Arthur saw the visit as an opportunity to speak to Charlotte and try to further his cause. After the evening service he followed her up the lane and tried to talk to her, but when this failed he hung back in the passageway to try again to get her on her own. She avoided him by going upstairs and Martha, spying from the kitchen door, saw him giving the retreating Charlotte 'flaysome looks'. He could not, or did not bother, to hide his disappointment and was so obviously dejected that the Bishop noticed it. Arthur let his temper show in one or two remarks to Patrick and annoyed Charlotte by his gloomy appearance. The 'little Bishop' soon realised the cause of Arthur's behaviour – it was a case of unrequited love. He felt sympathy for him, and, when the time came to leave, singled Arthur out particularly and left him with a kind word and a firm handshake. For Arthur it was a great relief to leave the tension of the Parsonage and return to his lodgings.

Shortly after this the inspector of schools arrived. Again hospitality had to be provided at the Parsonage and again Arthur must be there. This time he managed to get into a stupid and needless argument with the visitor, a confrontation which stirred up all Charlotte's old feelings about contentious curates and made her feel the sooner he left the better. In the time leading up to Easter Charlotte was very busy with the social affairs of the parish and had no time to think of sulky curates.

Arthur, on the other hand, was still considering his missionary application. He had seen no sign of peaceful overtures from Mr Brontë and no encouragement from Charlotte. A decision had to be made and, in spite of the lack of hopeful signs in Haworth, on 1st April he wrote to the U.S.P.G. to withdraw his application, excusing himself on the grounds that, 'the rheumatic affliction with which I have been troubled during the winter has not abated as quickly as I expected.' He thanked them for their trouble and, leaving himself an escape route, hoped that, if he wished to renew his application at some future date, they would look upon it with similar consideration. Arthur and Patrick were still not speaking. Joseph Grant and some of his fellow curates visited him as he sat in his dreary room and tried to cheer him up, but he hardly spoke to them, much less confided in them. He still let Flossy go to his room, sometimes took her for a walk, and, occasionally, walked over to Hebden Bridge to visit Sutcliffe Sowden, a round trip over the moors of some 20 miles. Perhaps he thought the hard physical exercise would take his mind off his problems. He felt and looked ill, never realising that Charlotte was aware of his plight but only dared to pity him from a distance. They never met or spoke and she observed that nobody seemed to like him: even if he were dying no one would speak a friendly word to him. In a quandary about his true character, she wrote, 'How much of all of this he deserves I can't tell – certainly he was never agreeable or amiable – and is now less than ever – and alas! I do not know him well enough to be sure there is truth and true affection – or only rancour and corroding disappointment at the bottom of his chagrin. In this state of things I must be and I am <u>entirely passive</u>. I may be losing the purest gem, and to me far the most precious life can give – genuine attachment – or I may be escaping the yoke of a morose temper.'[8]

Arthur found the violence of Patrick Brontë's reaction to his proposal puzzling in the extreme. He had served him diligently for eight years, and yet it seemed his loyalty counted for nothing. Did Patrick feel that he was too poor and insignificant to marry Charlotte now she was a famous author? Was he annoyed that

Arthur had broken with convention by not seeking permission from him before he proposed? As he tried to find the explanation, perhaps, in his misery, Arthur had overlooked the fact the Patrick Brontë was a frightened old man – frightened of loneliness if his only remaining child moved away and frightened that Charlotte was not physically strong enough for the childbearing marriage would bring. He never considered this: all he knew was that he had fallen in love with Charlotte Brontë the woman, not Currer Bell the author, and her father was a stumbling block in his path.

Unable to cope with the worsening atmosphere any longer Charlotte left to visit Mrs Gaskell in Manchester and then Ellen at Brookroyd. Meanwhile, Patrick was seeking a new curate and Arthur a new curacy. There was just about a month left when Charlotte returned before Arthur would leave. But on Whit Sunday, the week before he went, an event occurred which made Charlotte think she was being punished for her doubts of the true nature of Mr Nicholls.

He was taking the service that day and was surprised when Charlotte stayed for Communion. He was not prepared for this, thinking she would prefer not to come into such close contact with him. As she knelt before him his nerve completely failed. He struggled on until he faltered and then broke down altogether. He stood there, in front of the communicants, white, shaking and helpless. Joseph Redman, the Parish Clerk, tried to calm him down, and with a great effort he managed to whisper and falter his way through to the end of the service. By this time many of the women in the congregation were sobbing and Charlotte herself was in tears. Mr Brontë was not present at the service, much to Charlotte's relief, but word about what had taken place soon reached him. He condemned Arthur for an unmanly driveller, but Charlotte was convinced that his feelings for her were deep and genuine.

No official reason had been given for Arthur's leaving and the churchwardens convened a meeting with him, determined to find out what had been going on. Why was he leaving – was it his fault or Mr Brontë's? Arthur replied that it was his own. They wanted to know whether he blamed Patrick. He answered that, if it was anyone's fault, it was his own. Next they asked if he wanted to go. He said he did not want to leave and that it gave him great pain. Whatever else might have been thought of him at this time he was loyal to his superior. The churchwardens had no choice but to be content with his responses to their questioning, and matters took their inevitable course. The Saturday morning tutoring had to cease and one of his pupils, John Robinson, recalled in old age that it was Mr Nicholls who taught him what love-sickness really meant. He had heard him moan with anguish when things did not run smoothly. Charlotte was fully aware of his suffering, remembering perhaps how she had suffered from her unrequited love of M. Heger, and felt deeply distressed. However, as a dutiful daughter, she must obey papa. She continued the story to Ellen: 'I never saw a battle more sternly fought with the feelings than Mr N--- fights with his – and when he yields momentarily – you are almost sickened by the sense of strain upon him. However, he is to go – and I cannot speak to him or look at him or comfort him a whit – and I must submit. Providence is over all – that is the only consolation.'⁹

At the Whitsuntide school tea, which Patrick and Arthur both had to attend, Arthur, possibly fearing further sarcasm, actually snubbed Mr Brontë when he attempted to speak to him. This public insult did nothing to help his case and made Patrick more bitter than ever. Even so, sympathy had swung round much more in Arthur's favour and the parishioners were organising a public subscription to buy a farewell gift, a gold watch, engraved with the inscription, 'Presented to the Rev. A.B.Nicholls, B.A. by the teachers, scholars and congregation of St Michael's, Haworth, Yorkshire. May 25th 1853.'¹⁰ The presentation took place in the National School before a large gathering including local gentry and clergy. Significantly, it did not include the Rev. Patrick Brontë who pleaded ill health and pointedly stayed away. The presentation was made by Michael Merrall, Treasurer of the Mechanics' Institute and member of a well-known mill-owning family, who spoke well of Arthur and regretted his going. In spite of his dejection, the ceremony, and the thought given to it, must have been of some consolation and satisfaction .

The next day, Sunday, was his last 'working' day and he realised he would have to take the services. The 'illness' of Patrick caused him this unnecessary anguish and Charlotte told Ellen he should not have had to do it. After his breakdown at the Communion Service the previous week, he found his last services a 'cruel struggle', but nevertheless managed them without mishap. He returned to his lodgings to make sure all his paperwork was in order to hand over to Mr Brontë the following evening, including the deeds of the National School which, considering the effort he had put into its improvement, must have been a sad wrench. However, the die had been cast, a new curate appointed and he had to face the fact that he was leaving. On Monday he arrived at the Parsonage to find spring cleaning in full swing. The servants were washing the paint in the dining room where Charlotte usually sat. He looked in, hoping to see her there, but she had thought it best to keep out of the way, and had no intention of going into her father's study to speak to him in her father's presence. Arthur handed over the documents and hung about as long as he possibly could, hoping to see her, but, when it became obvious he would not, he said his farewells and left. She was watching and saw that he was lingering in the garden. She changed her mind, took her courage in both hands and, trembling with nervousness, went out to see him. Arthur, in his disappointment and grief, was leaning up against the garden door in a 'paroxysm of anguish, sobbing as women never sob'.[11] He could not have done anything better to win her over. She went straight up to him, forgetting anything she wanted to ask him, to give him comfort. He wanted hope and encouragement and, although she could not give it in quite such measure as he wanted, she showed she was not indifferent to his devotion and unhappiness. They spoke very few words and Arthur turned and hurried back to Sexton House. He packed his bag and at 6 am the next morning left Haworth.

Courtship and Wedding

Two days later, Rev. George de Renzy, appointed in Arthur's place, performed his first duties. He was a tall, thin, pale young man, quite the opposite of Nicholls' dark colouring and sturdy build. After eight years service in Haworth, Arthur was thoroughly familiar with the running of the parish and needed no guidance: to de Renzy everything was new, and help and instruction were needed. Mr Brontë, who had not had to train a new curate for some years, had forgotten just how burdensome this could be, and in his old age he was becoming increasingly impatient. Although desperately in need of help, he did not like his new assistant.

Charlotte was unhappy and lonely. Now Arthur had gone she began to think about what she had refused and wondered if a life of spinsterhood, with no one save her father for company, was what she really wanted. She had no idea where Arthur was going, other than that he was spending some time away before he took up a curacy elsewhere. She might never hear from him or see him again. To make matters worse, she caught influenza and was in bed for ten days. She had not long recovered when the very thing she had dreaded happened – her father had another stroke. For a time he became completely blind. Although Mr Brontë slowly recovered, his sight was never completely restored and, more than ever, he needed the help of his curate. Mr de Renzy was often lax in his duties, perhaps because he did not understand fully what was expected of him. The parishioners did not like him and Charlotte herself could not help comparing him unfavourably with Arthur. Ellen noticed her changed attitude towards Nicholls and did not like it: she appeared jealous of the threat to their close relationship. The friendship cooled and it was not until Charlotte was making arrangements for her wedding that it regained its former warmth.

Yet Arthur was not giving up hope so easily. He wrote to her to tell her that he was taking a curacy at Kirk Smeaton, near Pontefract, in August, and he begged her to write to him.

Stealthily she read the letter out of sight of her father but made no reply. Arthur was disappointed when he received no answer, though by now he had overcome his nervousness and, nothing daunted, wrote again. Still there was no reply, but he was not to be put off. Five times he wrote, with no answer forthcoming, but on the sixth time at last came a short note. In it Charlotte exhorted him, 'to heroic submission to his lot'. It was just what he wanted. It gave him an opening to further correspondence and, with a deviousness quite unlike his earlier behaviour, Arthur wrote that the letter had given him such comfort that he must have a little more. His tactics worked and, before long, they were in regular correspondence. Charlotte was in a dilemma: for the first time ever she was disobeying and deceiving her father.

In July, 1853, unknown to Mr Brontë, Arthur had been to stay with his friend Joseph Grant,[1] the curate of Oxenhope, at the Grammar School at Marsh,[2] less than a mile from the Parsonage, maybe hoping for a glimpse of Charlotte.

The church at Kirk Smeaton, near Pontefract, to which Arthur had been appointed was St Mary's (now re-dedicated to St.Peter), within the Deanery of Doncaster, part of the Archdiocese of York, and in the patronage of Earl Fitzwilliam. It was a well endowed living and the Rector, Rev. Thomas Cator, was a wealthy man who needed a curate to take charge when he was away visiting his many friends. Arthur arrived in August to find the work load very light, especially compared with his busy life at Haworth. The church building, with a minstrel gallery and tub-like pews, was in need of some restoration, there was no organ and the singing was led by two violinists.[3] Here he found plenty of time and peace for his jangled nerves to steady and to plan his campaign to win over Charlotte.

She, in the meantime, went on a visit to Scotland, with the Taylors but their child became ill and, after only a few days, she returned. She found her father peevish, depressed and as vituperative towards Arthur as before. Even so, when Arthur made another visit to Oxenhope, he and Charlotte managed to meet. They continued writing to each other but Charlotte was feeling more guilty than ever. Perhaps in an effort to run away from her conscience, she went visiting again – this time to her old teacher and friend, Miss Wooler, at Ilkley. While she was away, a letter, addressed to her, arrived at the Parsonage, and, probably suspecting it was from Nicholls, Mr Brontë opened it. It was from Mrs Gaskell, saying she would shortly arrive to stay for a few days. Charlotte came home the next day and the atmosphere was not improved by the fact that she was furious with Papa for opening her private correspondence. During the four days Elizabeth Gaskell was at Haworth, she drew Charlotte out to talk about her life, chatting for hours over the fire in the evenings and during their walks over the moors. She was told about Arthur and sympathised with Charlotte's predicament. The visit was a great success and Arthur had won a supporter.

Mrs Gaskell thought Mr Brontë's opposition was due to Arthur's lack of money and influential friends; she was resolved to help and, not short of influential friends herself, she discussed Arthur's position with Richard Monckton Milnes, a rich socialite and patron of the arts.[4] She did not wish Arthur or Charlotte to know what was afoot as they might have resented her interference. To Monckton Milnes on 29th October,1853 she wrote:

'With skilful diplomacy, for which I admire myself extremely, I have obtained the address we want.
    The revd A. B. Nicholls,
        Kirk Smeaton near
            Pontefract,
                Yorkshire
. . . I felt sure you would keep my story secret, – if my well-meant treachery becomes known to her I shall lose her friendship , which I prize most highly.'[5]

Fryston Hall, near Castleford, was only some eight miles from Kirk Smeaton, and shortly Monckton Milnes called on Arthur. This was no doubt partly out of his own curiosity, partly to report back to Mrs Gaskell, but also to offer him other possible posts. These offers he had arranged with the help of Dr Hook, Vicar of Leeds, who had wide patronage. Arthur, bemused at this interest in his affairs, was offered a choice of two posts. One was in Lancashire, and one in Scotland, both of which he declined as he knew that to win Charlotte he would have to stay at Haworth. One wonders how genuine these offers were or whether they were a test of his resolve.

Monckton Milnes wrote giving his impressions of Arthur to Mrs Gaskell, who at that time had only heard about him from Charlotte and had never seen him:[6]

'He is a strong built, somewhat hard featured sort of man, with a good deal of Celtic sentiment about his manner and voice – quite the type of the Northern Irishman. He seemed sadly in broken spirits and declined two cures which Dr Hook had enabled me to offer him . . . He gave the impression of a man whose ardour was burnt out. I was amused at his surprise at the interest I took in him and carefully avoided any mention of you. He spoke with great respect of Mr Brontë's abilities and character and of her simply and unreservedly.' She replied, enclosing a letter from Charlotte,[7] and saying, 'I think that the enclosed letter will give you true pleasure . . . I can't help fancying your kind words may have made him feel he was not so friendless as he represented himself and believed himself to be at first; and might rouse his despondency up to a fresh effort.'[8]

Apart from the offer of other livings, Mrs Gaskell had discussed with Monckton Milnes the possibility of a pension to Charlotte or Arthur from one of the many charities with which he had some sway. Her letter of 29th October had continued, 'I have been thinking over little bits of the conversation we had relating to a pension. I do not think she would take it; I am quite sure that one hundred a year given as an acknowledgement of his merits as a good faithful clergyman would give her ten times the pleasure that two hundred would do, if bestowed upon her in her capacity as a writer . . .'

Later in June, 1854, she wrote, 'I could not wait or run the chance of seeing you before thanking you most truly about Mr Nicholls. I am sure you will keep the secret: and if you want a steam-engine or 1,000 yards of calico pray employ me in Manchester'[9] The implication seems to be that a pension was arranged but we cannot be certain whether Arthur actually received any money or not.

Charlotte, feeling very flat and alone after Mrs Gaskell's departure, soon set off to renew her visit to Miss Wooler, now staying in Hornsea. She had much to occupy her mind. The short secret meetings she had with Arthur, when she walked along Walled Lane, the flagged path to Oxenhope; his letters to read out of Papa's sight; Ellen's attitude towards her; all were causing her agitation. Relations with her father were still strained and, on her return, she decided to go to London. On the November day she was making arrangements for her trip, a letter arrived from George Smith. It was so strange that she was perturbed, thinking that something was the matter, and wondered whether he was ill. She wrote to his mother for an explanation and she replied telling her that George was engaged to be married to Elizabeth Blakeway, the beautiful, young, rich daughter of a London wine merchant. He had met her at a ball and it was love at first sight. Any hopes Charlotte had entertained in his direction were completely dashed. She immediately cancelled her trip to London and returned a box of books with instructions that no more were to be sent. Her note of congratulation to George on 10th December was curt in the extreme: 'My dear Sir, in great happiness, as in great grief – accept my meed of congratulations, – and believe me sincerely yours, C.Brontë.'[10] If Arthur did but know it, another obstacle was removed from his path.

Fortunately, he was again at Oxenhope and would probably see Charlotte when she was at her most vulnerable. He could offer her love, security and loyalty. He had not the charisma of Heger or the sophistication of Smith, but he had tenacity and faithfulness. Although she was not yet in love with him, she began to feel that these were qualities which she would be foolish to disregard. Her father was becoming impossible in his attitude: the thought of living alone with him like that for the rest of his life was not to be contemplated. She had grown to admire the good qualities in Arthur: she could give him the hope he wanted; his love was too good to be thrown away by someone as lonely as she was. If they could gain Mr Brontë's consent, they would be married.

Now it was her turn to work out the tactics they would use. The first was to confess that she was in contact with Arthur. She plucked up courage and told Papa everything. It was she later told Ellen, 'Hard and rough work at the time – but the issue after a few days was that I had obtained leave to continue the communication.'[11] She asked for the right to be able to get to know Arthur better and this Mr Brontë grudgingly granted, though he must have known that, if he withheld his permission, Charlotte, having decided her course, with or without his consent, would pursue it. She could be just as stubborn as he was.

Arthur was due to come to Oxenhope in January, 1854. He stayed with the Grants again, this time for ten days, and was now free to meet Charlotte openly. The weather, however, was atrocious and he had to walk over deep frozen snow to the Parsonage and his beloved. Mr Brontë deigned to receive him, but not pleasantly. He was still resentful and did not enjoy seeing Arthur looking happier, but the more Charlotte saw of Arthur the better she liked him and, given time, they hoped to win the old man round.

After Arthur had returned to Kirk Smeaton, whether consciously or not, Charlotte began to work subtly on her father. De Renzy was getting more and more on Patrick's nerves, often missing services and putting Patrick to the trouble of bringing in other clergy to fill the gaps. He complained that he needed an active and dedicated curate, and Charlotte would have been less than perspicacious if she could not have turned such talk to her advantage. She subtly emphasised Arthur's qualities and secretly blessed de Renzy for his attitude. Arthur continued to correspond and together, he and Charlotte, decided that if they were to suggest to Mr Brontë that, after marriage, they would remain at the Parsonage, he could live out the rest of his life with them. This, of course, depended on Arthur resuming the curacy at Haworth. In this way everyone would be satisfied without loss of face; except, of course, de Renzy!

There is no record of Arthur being licensed to the curacy of Kirk Smeaton, but the Rector and the Bishop of Ripon had to be consulted about the possibility of his returning to Haworth. When this had been arranged, Arthur came over again on 3rd April and stayed till the following Friday.[12] Mr Brontë, suffering from bronchitis, was tired and ill, and Arthur and Charlotte again took advantage of the situation and explained their plans for the future. They assured Patrick that he should still have his privacy, they would disturb none of the domestic arrangements, Arthur would have a study of his own and contribute to the expenses of housekeeping, and they would look after him in his declining years and, whatever happened, he would not be left alone. Arthur would relieve him of the main burden of parish duties and Charlotte would ensure his physical comfort. He would be rid of de Renzy and all would continue much as before.

With such a rosy picture of the future, the sick old man at last swallowed his objections and his pride and gave his consent to their engagement. Arthur was triumphant, Charlotte thoughtful and Mr Brontë satisfied. It was a different Arthur who returned light-heartedly to Kirk Smeaton to celebrate Palm Sunday, leaving Charlotte to inform her friends of her change of status. Yet her letters were not those of a woman passionately in love and, if Arthur could have read them, he would have surely felt that something was missing.[13] 'I am still very calm – very inexpectant, what I taste of happiness is of the soberest order. I trust to love my husband – I am grateful to him for his tender love to me – Providence offers me this destiny. Doubtless it is then the best for me . . .' she wrote to Ellen. In her letter to Mrs Gaskell she again speaks of her gratitude to Arthur – not exactly the response he hoped to wake in her.

George Smith, her publisher, who had heard the news of her engagement, wrote to congratulate her, and Charlotte replied in a strange, wistful letter: 'My expectations are very subdued – very different I daresay to what yours were when you were married. Care and fear stand so close to hope that I can sometimes scarcely see her for the shadows they cast. And yet I am thankful too and the doubtful future must be left with providence.
I hardly know in what form to include your wife's name, as I have never seen her. Say to her whatever may seem to you most appropriate and most expressive of goodwill.
In the course of the year that's gone Cornhill and London have receded a long way from me; the links of communication have waxed very frail and few. It must be so in this world. All things considered I would not wish it otherwise.'[14]

She asked Mr Metcalfe, her solicitor, to arrange for the transfer of her stocks in the funds from George Smith, who had been managing her investments for her. This was indeed the end of the intimacy between Cornhill and their celebrated author.

Arthur had his own friends to acquaint with his happy news and was in much greater spirits than his bride-to-be. He was also busy making arrangements for leaving Kirk Smeaton and returning to Haworth. De Renzy had to be informed and a new curacy procured for him. All would have to be done quickly if the wedding was to take place in the summer as he planned. He wished the honeymoon to be spent in Ireland so he could show off his new wife to his Irish relatives. Mr Brontë had never wholly believed him when he had described his home there, thinking it was a figment of his imagination, or at least a gross exaggeration. Now there was a chance to prove his story.

Back at the Parsonage, domestic arrangements had to be made in order to fulfil the couple's promise to live there and to allow Mr Brontë his privacy. Arthur, of course, being a man and a curate, must have a study of his own: there was no suggestion that Charlotte, now a famous author, should have one too. Some time before, when her writing had brought her some money, Charlotte had provided window blinds and damask curtains, Kidderminster carpets, rugs and a stair-carpet, to add to the comfort of the house. Now she decided that the peat store behind the dining room would be converted into her husband's study. Workmen arrived and began the alterations. She chose a green and white colour scheme for the wall-paper and curtains, which she made herself. The cost of the work was over £10 – about £1,000 in today's money – but it would ensure Arthur his own private space.

Life was becoming increasingly busy. There were letters to be replied to, as well as written, and pre-wedding visits to be made, not forgetting the actual marriage arrangements. Charlotte's 'Charming little Bishop' wrote with his congratulations which pleased both her and her father.[15] He expressed 'so cordial an approbation of Mr Nicholl's return to Haworth and such kind gratification at the domestic arrangements which are to ensue'. He had, it appeared, discovered the state of things when he was there in January, 1853 – while his benevolence sympathised with Mr N – then in 'sorrow and dejection'. The Gaskells invited Charlotte and Arthur to pay them a visit, and though Charlotte happily accepted she did not pass on the invitation to Arthur, giving as an excuse that it might unsettle him. It is more likely she was afraid his Puseyite views would upset the Unitarian Gaskells and lose her a good friend. Whilst there, Catherine and Emily Winkworth came over and they enjoyed a good gossip. When Catherine, prompted by 'Lily' Gaskell, asked her about her fiancé, the conversation took on a more serious tone. Charlotte said that she could not conceal from herself that Arthur was not intellectual and there were many places into which he could not follow her intellectually. She confessed that the fact that Arthur was High Church might cause some awkwardness among some of her friends, but he would not turn her into a bigot. When Catherine suggested to Charlotte that she could perhaps change his attitude, she replied, 'That is what I hope. He has a sincere love of goodness wherever he sees it. I think if he could come to know Mr Gaskell he would change his feeling.' This short visit and meeting with her friends did much to calm her pre-nuptial nerves. Later Catherine Winkworth perceptively observed that she would probably be 'much more really happy' with a man like Arthur, than with someone who might have made her more in love.[16]

Arthur had also been invited to visit Joe and Amelia Taylor at Hunsworth with Charlotte and to Brookroyd to see Ellen Nussey. Because of Mr Cator's stipulation that his curate must be at Kirk Smeaton when he was away, Arthur had to refuse. Mr Cator was spending some weeks in Town with his family, so Charlotte made these two visits again on her own. At Brookroyd she told Ellen that she wished her to be her bridesmaid, and the wedding would be very quiet. It was almost a year since she had last been there, and during the visit any remaining bad feelings between the friends were submerged in wedding plans. Ellen helped Charlotte to chose her trousseau in Halifax and Leeds. On Charlotte's insistence, the clothes had to be inexpensive, serviceable and able to be 'turned to decent use after the wedding day'.

On her return to Haworth, on 13th May, she found that her father had given de Renzy his marching orders. Not surprisingly, de Renzy was upset and annoyed, although no doubt he had seen this coming. He wrote a very unpleasant letter to Arthur and went behind Patrick's back, complaining to anyone who would listen to him about his treatment. Yet in front of Patrick he was perfectly 'smooth and fair spoken'. In a letter to Ellen , Charlotte complained, '. . . for his own sake and his office sake I wish he would be quiet.' On the contrary, he started to make difficulties about the date of his departure, upsetting all the wedding plans and making Charlotte furious. She had wanted the ceremony to be in July but this had to be altered. Mr Brontë had already said that de Renzy could have three weeks of paid leave but he was now sticking out for a further fortnight more in the pretence of wanting a holiday. 'Papa has every legal right to frustrate this at once by telling him he must stay till his quarter is up – I feel compelled to throw the burden of the contest upon Mr Nicholls who is younger – more pugnacious and can bear it better. The worst of it is Mr N. has not Papa's right to speak and act or he would do it to purpose.'[17] Arthur was already being regarded as a hedge against trouble for the Brontë household and was seen by Charlotte as not just a talker but a man of deeds.

While Charlotte had been away, Arthur had not been feeling well and thought it was the return of his old rheumatic trouble. When he arrived at Haworth on 23rd May, despite the fact that Mr Cator was still away, Charlotte was worried by his appearance. She questioned him about his illness but gradually felt relieved when, 'In the first place he could give me no name'. He told her he felt so ill, he thought he was going to die, but she told him in no uncertain terms that people who were going to die did not travel fifty miles to tell you so! It was just what he needed, a good dose of common sense to steady his nerves. He had been to see Mr Teale, who also assured him that he could find nothing wrong except that he was overwrought. While he was at Haworth he had good wholesome treatment and soon felt better. He stayed until the following Saturday during which time the details of Charlotte's Marriage Settlement were arranged.[18]

In the days before the Married Women's Property Act was passed, a marriage settlement was quite normal as, after marriage, a woman could not own anything in her own right: everything became the property of her husband. Usually the money in the settlement came from the bride's family but in this case from savings made from Charlotte's earnings. Joe Taylor was appointed the sole Trustee and the amount, £1,678, was invested in 3¼% reduced Bank Annuities. Under the terms of the Settlement, she was to receive the income each year for her personal use. If Arthur died first, the capital would be paid to Charlotte and the trust wound up. If Charlotte died first and had children, the funds would be paid out in equal shares as each came of age. If she died leaving no issue, the funds were to go to her father. Her solicitor, Richard Metcalfe, came to the Parsonage with the deed, which was signed and sealed by Joe Taylor, Charlotte and Arthur and witnessed by Patrick and Mr Metcalfe on 24th May, 1854.

Mr de Renzy had managed to persuade Patrick to allow him the extra two weeks holiday and he was to leave on June 25th, Arthur was to leave Kirk Smeaton on the 11th and the wedding was to be on June 29th. Arthur, responsible for arranging substitute clergy during his absence, succeeded in persuading de Renzy to return for some services and turned to Joseph Grant of Oxenhope, William Mayne, curate of Ingrow, and Thomas Crowther to assist Patrick. He returned to Kirk Smeaton in a better frame of mind.

Charlotte insisted that Arthur kept the marriage arrangements as secret as possible and he, 'being a kind considerate fellow, with all his masculine faults in some points – enters into my wishes about having the thing done quietly'. To avoid the embarrassment of having the banns called, arranged for a

Special Licence. Charlotte was compiling a list of people who should receive wedding announcement cards; her own list consisted of 18 names. Ellen was in charge of ordering them and Charlotte thought 50 cards would be plenty, but when she received Arthur's list she was amazed to see the number on it. She had no idea he had 'such a string of clerical acquaintance,' there seemed 'no end to his string of parson friends,' and she immediately asked Ellen to double the order. In this flurry of preparations, Arthur decided he would come and spend a week with her in Haworth and she was thoroughly provoked. She was trying to finish her sewing and told him she could not possibly put up with him for a whole week. Arthur, having now recovered from his dose of pre-wedding, nerves was now getting a taste of hers. Sensibly he stayed only a few days and then gave his mind to organising the travel arrangements for Ellen and Miss Wooler, who were the only two people Charlotte had invited to the ceremony. He anticipated the arrangements she was going to suggest and Charlotte wrote to Margaret Wooler: 'Mr N- requires knowing to be appreciated – and I must say I have not yet found him to lose with closer knowledge – I make no great discoveries – but I occasionally come on a quiet little nook of character, which excites esteem. He is always reliable, truthful, faithful, affectionate, a little unbending perhaps, but still persuadable and opened to kind influence. A man never indeed to be driven – but who may be led.'[19] It was a brilliant summing-up of his character.

Arthur had arranged the wedding for eight o'clock on the morning of Thursday, 29th June, 1854. His old friend Sutcliffe Sowden would conduct the service and Ellen and Miss Wooler would accompany Charlotte.[20] The day before, the two ladies would arrive at Keighley on the same train and would be driven the four miles to the Parsonage in a cab. Arthur and Sutcliffe would stay overnight with the ever-helpful Joseph Grant. The Grants were not asked to the ceremony itself but to the wedding breakfast afterwards. In deference to Charlotte's wishes Arthur could hardly have arranged a simpler ceremony.

Charlotte in Haworth and Arthur in Oxenhope were both up early, she to put on her wedding dress and he to walk across the field path to the church. The morning was cloudy and quiet. Outside the Parsonage, John Robinson, the same boy who recalled Arthur's lovesickness, was dawdling in the lane. John Brown saw him and told him to go to the top of the hill and look out for three men.[21] As soon as he spotted them he was to run to the Parsonage and give them the news. As they came into sight he recognised them – Joseph Grant, Sutcliffe Sowden and his former tutor Arthur Nicholls and realised something interesting was about to take place. According to instructions he passed on his news, and was told to bring Joseph Redman, the Parish Clerk, to the church. Having done this, he lingered on and, as he was later to recall in old age, saw Miss Brontë and her friends walking down the path to the church.

Arthur and Sutcliffe stood in the doorway to greet the bridal party. As they approached, Arthur was worried to see Mr Brontë was not with them . There was Charlotte herself, Miss Wooler and Ellen Nussey but of the father-of-the-bride no sign. The evening before he had told Charlotte that he could not attend. As usual he pleaded ill health, but for some time he had been refusing to conduct weddings and seemed to have developed a superstitious fear of the ceremony. Whether it was that, or whether he was still not sure that Charlotte was taking the right step, he flatly refused to be present. To Arthur's relief, Miss Wooler deputised for Patrick and gave Charlotte away. The couple signed the Register in the vestry and left the church by the side door as man and wife. This momentous step in their lives was achieved in a very few minutes.

In spite of their trying to keep the wedding secret, news had got around, and a small crowd of villagers saw Charlotte in her white muslin wedding dress leave the church as Mrs Arthur Nicholls. Some described her as looking 'like a snowdrop'. A white bonnet decorated with green leaves and a white lace mantle completed her simple costume, a total contrast to Arthur's dark clerical clothes. The small party arrived back at the Parsonage to be greeted by Martha. The house had been decorated with flowers and the wedding breakfast was laid out in the dining room for eight guests. Mr Brontë had made a remarkable recovery; far from being unwell, he was described by Martha as the life and soul of the party, behaving very well in his grandiloquent manner. Ellen scattered flowers on the table and everyone had an enjoyable time. Charlotte retired to change into her going-away outfit of grey-mauve shot silk with a grey cashmere shawl and a grey bonnet trimmed with pink roses. The couple went outside and John Robinson, still lurking in the lane, saw them drive off in a carriage and pair to Keighley station on the first stage of their honeymoon.

Honeymoon

They arrived at the pillared portico of Keighley Station after the drive from Haworth, with Arthur feeling pride and relief and Charlotte feeling full of cold! They passed through the booking hall to the platform behind. Arthur had arranged everything – the tickets, the time table, the luggage.[1] All Charlotte had to do was relax. Already she was feeling the difference between having to organise everything herself and leaving it all to Arthur, who had obviously given a great deal of thought to their honeymoon itinerary, the first stage of which would take them to Conway, North Wales. Long train journeys were still something of an adventure, especially as the trains had no facilities on board. Passengers had to take their chance at finding cloakrooms, or food, when they changed trains or stopped at stations en route – a formidable task if the stop was short and the train crowded.

They settled into their compartment, still reminiscent of the interior of a stage coach.[2] Modern day travellers would deplore the upright wooden seats with their strip of thin upholstery to sit on but it was normal for the time and no one thought anything of it. Even so, Arthur would do his best to ensure she had a good seat with a view and was as comfortable as possible – far more so than those who travelled third class. The weather was fair with patchy sunshine and the journey quite pleasant, which was just as well as it would include three changes and take most of the day.[3]

At last they glimpsed their first sight of the Castle across the River Conway and rumbled through Stephenson's tubular bridge into the station,[4] not far from the hotel where Arthur had arranged for them to stay.[5] Although the weather had turned wet and windy, as they walked up the ramp from the station, they would see before them the towers of the Town Walls climbing the hill. They hurried over the cobbled street, a porter wheeling their luggage rattling behind, to the Castle Hotel. Arthur proudly signed the visitors' book, the first time in public to write his wife's new name.[6] The hotel was comfortable and Charlotte wrote a note to Ellen to assure her that they had arrived safely, and that her cold was no worse. In spite of the weather they spent a very pleasant day in Conway before moving on to Bangor, the railway line following the coastline of Conway Bay with Penmaenmawr Mountain dominating the scene.

Their remaining time was spent driving out on excursions to places of grandeur and beauty. One such drive was through the dramatic pass of Llanberis to the little village of Beddgelert. The village is situated by the confluence of two rivers in a peaceful valley surrounded by towering mountains and was even then being developed as a tourist resort with the substantial Goat Hotel for visitors. Travelling by horse and carriage they would not have had time to return daily to Conway or Bangor and, if they stayed anywhere in the district, it was likely they would have stayed there. The Hotel was known to Sir James Kay-Shuttleworth, who had entertained Charlotte at Gawthorpe, as his younger brother Thomas had married the landlord's daughter.[7] Apart from the magnificent panorama, there was an old church to visit, and Gelert's grave. According to legend, Gelert had been left to guard the son of his master, Llewelyn the Great.[8] When Llewelyn had returned he found the dog covered in blood and, thinking it had attacked his son, killed it. Later the baby was found alive and the blood was from a wolf which Gelert had killed to save the child. The dog was buried in a field south of the village and Llewelyn had a large stone erected in memory of his faithful hound. Charlotte was delighted with the trip and Arthur must have been pleased at the success of his plans. To Catherine Wooler, Margaret's sister, Charlotte wrote that she had seen some splendid scenery and it 'surpassed anything I remember of the English Lakes'. Arthur had arranged for them to be in Holyhead on Tuesday, 4th July, to catch the packet to Ireland, so they could not linger but rejoined the train to cross the Menai Straits and Anglesey.[9]

At Holyhead, the station was at the end of the harbour but there was an extension line of almost a mile to the Admiralty Pier from which the packet boats left. The engines were uncoupled at the station because the line was unsuitable for locomotives and each coach was drawn by horses on to the pier. The tight curves caused the wheels to screech against the lines and, as the coaches went on their way, the local boys used to run alongside, cheering them on and hoping passengers would throw pennies to them.[10] Like the other passengers, Arthur and Charlotte would have been captivated by this new experience. On the pier the passengers alighted, crossed the few yards to the south side and boarded the ship.

The packet boats were paddle steamers, usually with a single funnel. They were small, carrying up to 250 passengers, although one had brought over 300 on a visit to the Great Exhibition in 1851. There were sofas provided for the ladies but not enough seats for all. The crossing took around five hours for the 60 miles but depended greatly on the weather. For Arthur and Charlotte the sea was calm and they had a smooth and uneventful crossing. They had their first sight of Ireland as they passed the peninsula of Howth with its prominent hill. Crossing Dublin Bay they came into the arms of the new large harbour of Kingstown[11] and landed at Victoria Wharf, a stone's throw away from the railway station from where the trains left for the five-mile run to Dublin.[12]

On their arrival there they were met by three of Arthur's relatives – his brother Alan, his 23-year-old cousin Joseph and his favourite cousin, Mary Anna. Much to Arthur's satisfaction, Charlotte was impressed. Exactly what she had expected his family to be like can only be guessed. She wrote to Margaret Wooler, 'Three of Mr Nicholls relatives met us in Dublin – his brother and two cousins. The first (brother) is manager of the Grand Canal from Dublin to Banagher;[13] a sagacious, well informed and courteous man. His cousin is a student and has just gained three Premiums. The other cousin was a pretty, ladylike girl, with gentle English manners.' Unknown to any of them, Charlotte had just met the girl who would eventually take her place and become Arthur's second wife. The plan was to stay in Dublin for a short break, before going on to Banagher and the Bell family home. In the event Charlotte's cold became much worse and they stayed only two days.

In that time Arthur showed her many of the places which were familiar to him from his student days. He took her to Trinity College, where they entered through the archway, with its domed ceiling and unusual floor of hexagonal wooden blocks, into Front Square. Before them, a new sight for Arthur as well as Charlotte, was the 90 feet high Campanile, erected only the previous year. Beyond was The Rubrics, the College's oldest building, where Arthur had had his lodgings. He particularly wished her to see the Chapel, with its beautiful stucco ceiling and richly patterned floor tiles; a building at the heart of Arthur's training to be a priest. The seating was in the 'collegiate' style so the congregation sat facing each other across the central aisle. Directly facing the Chapel and giving symmetry to Front Square was its 'twin' – the Examination Hall, with an organ said to have been rescued from a Spanish ship. No doubt Charlotte found it hard on her feet walking over the cobbled pathways to the Museum. Like the Campanile this had also been built since Arthur's days and it was as novel to him as to Charlotte. It was built in the Venetian style, highly ornamented with mouldings of leaves and flowers, berries and birds, all of which were different. There was as much interest to be had in the building itself as in the artefacts it exhibited. Its high domed mosaic ceiling, the varieties of marble in the staircase and its ornate pillars made it one of the most fascinating buildings in the College. If the Museum was one of the most fascinating buildings, the Library was one of the most beautiful. Some 240-feet-long with its restrained plaster-work ceiling and pillared bays, the shelves upon shelves of rare and costly books must have been a delight to Charlotte.

They spent further time driving around Dublin to look at the main sights, passing the many Georgian houses that make Dublin so elegant a city. They made calls on other Bell relatives, but by this time Charlotte was really exhausted. Her cold was even worse and she was in no condition for further sight-seeing. As she mentioned in her letter to Margaret Wooler, 'We would have seen much more – had not my cold been a restraint on us.' So, after two hectic days, on Friday 7th July, the little party set off by train for Banagher. At that time the railway only reached as far as Birr, seven miles from their destination, so from Birr station they drove to the top of the hill at Banagher and took an 'inside car' the half mile to Cuba Court.

As they entered through the iron gates, past the lodge and up the carriage drive, Arthur had his moment of triumph – now Charlotte could see the account of his upbringing had not been exaggerated – indeed she was not prepared for the sight of the large house standing in extensive grounds, with its flight of stone steps up to the imposing pilastered door. It was the residence of a well-to-do gentleman – grand and solid. The school buildings, Charlotte would later discover, ran behind the house.

As many of the Bell clan as possible were there to greet Arthur and his bride. Their hostess was Arthur's aunt and adoptive mother, the kind and practical Aunt Harriette. She saw at once how ill Charlotte was with her cold and cough and set about nursing her back to health. Their bedroom was a 'great room' on the ground floor, which would have looked gloomy but for a turf fire burning in the wide chimney. Here they could rest from the strain of their journey and Charlotte could recover her health. She wrote to Margaret Wooler, 'I was not well when I came here, fatigue and excitement had nearly knocked me up – and my cough had become very bad – but Mrs Bell nursed me with kindness and skill, and I am greatly better now.'[14]

As she improved she took more note of her surroundings, and, in her next letter, described them to Miss Wooler, 'I cannot help feeling singularly interested in all about the house. In this house Mr Nicholls was brought up by his uncle, Dr Bell. It is very large and looks externally like a gentleman's country seat – within, most of the rooms were lofty and spacious and some – the drawing room, the dining room, etc. handsomely and commodiously furnished.' However, the narrow passages caused by the layout of the rooms seemed to her desolate and bare.[15]

She relaxed in the presence of this warm hearted family and described them as being genteel and educated. 'The male members of the family – such as I have seen – seem thoroughly educated gentlemen. Mrs Bell is like an English or Scottish matron, quiet, kind and well bred – both her daughters are strikingly pretty in appearance – and their manners are very amiable and pleasing. I must say I like my new relations.' The tone of the letter shows that she was pleasantly surprised and one wonders what she had been expecting! Arthur appeared in a new light here on his home turf, surrounded by his family. Aunt Harriette spoke of him with affection and respect. Even some of the old servants told her that she was fortunate to have married one of the best gentlemen in the country. In fact, she heard nothing but praise for him, so much so that she now began to refer to him as 'my dear husband' and thanked God that she had made the right choice of partner. He was true, honourable and unboastful. At last she was happy and proud to be Mrs Arthur Nicholls.

They explored the grounds together and at the back of the house, next to the coach house and stable, saw the two-storey school block, with its ground-floor schoolroom where Arthur had obtained his education, and the dormitory above. The weather was warm, Cuba Court was peaceful and relaxing, their days were filled with walks with the family dogs, and excursions to nearby beauty spots. They both loved nature, enjoying the wild life and birds in the many trees, and watching the fishermen on the Shannon. In the evenings Charlotte often sat by the fire chatting with Mrs Bell. Arthur had the good sense to see that she relished these conversations and they did her good. They talked confidentially on so many topics so naturally that Mrs Bell herself said, 'Sitting together over the fire like this, I quite forget I am talking to the celebrated authoress!' In this pleasant fashion a week passed and it was time to move on.

They were to travel to Kilkee in County Clare on the west coast. Their journey took them along the banks of the beautiful River Shannon, past Lough Derg, one of Ireland's largest lakes to Limerick and then across country to their destination. Arthur had arranged lodgings at the second-best hotel in the little town, the West End Hotel.[16] A letter written from here to Catherine Wooler reveals just how relaxed Charlotte was feeling in his company. Together they could laugh at the drawbacks of the place. 'I had heard a great deal about Irish negligence etc. I own that until I came to Kilkee I saw little of it. Here at our inn – the splendidly designated West End Hotel – there is a good deal to carp at – if we were in a carping humour – but we laugh instead of grumbling for out of doors there is much to compensate for any indoor shortcomings; so magnificent an ocean – so bold and grand a coast – I never yet saw.'[17] Kilkee had a beautifully curved sandy bay guarded by strangely formed rocks and tall cliffs at either end, which the Atlantic rollers rushing in hit with spectacular effect. Arthur wrote to George Sowden, 'It was most refreshing to sit on a rock and look out at the broad Atlantic foaming at our feet.'[18] The first morning there the honeymooners escaped the slatternly attentions of Mrs Shannon, their landlady, and went out to watch the sea.

One of Charlotte's doubts before they were married was that Arthur would not let her look at things in her own way: in solitude and silence. Yet he understood her more than she realised. He let her sit on the cliffs where she wished, gave her a rug to keep off the spray and left her alone, only interrupting when he noticed her moving too close to the edge for safety. She confided to Catherine Winkworth, 'So far he is always good in this way – and this protection which does not interfere or pretend is, I believe, a thousand times better than any half sort of pseudo-sympathy. I will try with God's help to be as indulgent to him whenever indulgence is needed.'[19] So impressed were they that, despite the hotel, they made this the longest stop on their tour, and spent much of the time watching such fierce waves as Charlotte had never imagined.

From there they moved south, crossing the Shannon by ferry to Tarbert and on to Tralee and Killarney. Charlotte was thrilled and entranced as they explored the mountains, streams and lakes of Killarney and the Iveragh Peninsula. Having Arthur constantly on hand to guide and help her left her free to enjoy herself without the mundane worries of the tour. She appreciated his solicitude and as the days passed he rose in her estimation. They collected ferns, which Charlotte pressed in a book as a souvenir of their honeymoon.[20]

On a trip to the Gap of Dunloe an incident occurred which shook them both.[21] She described what happened in a letter to Catherine Winkworth, 'We saw and went through the Gap of Dunloe. A sudden glimpse of a very dim phantom came on us in the Gap.[22] The guide had warned me to alight from my horse as the path was now very broken and dangerous – I did not feel afraid and declined – we passed the dangerous part – the horse trembled in every limb and slipped once but did not fall – soon after, she (it was a mare) started and was unruly for a minute – however I kept my seat – my husband went to her head to lead her – suddenly without any apparent cause – she seemed to go mad – reared and plunged – I was thrown on the stones right under her – my husband did not see that I had fallen, he still held her – I saw and felt her kick, plunge, trample around me. I had my thoughts about the moment – its consequences – my husband – my father – when my plight was seen the struggling creature was let loose – she sprang over me. I was lifted off the stones neither bruised by the fall or touched by the horses hoofs (*sic*). Of course the only feeling left was gratitude for more sakes than my own.'[23] In the shock of the accident she had thought of Arthur before her father. The honeymoon was obviously proving the success her husband had hoped.

From Killarney they continued south through the mountains to Glengarriff. Its sheltered position at the head of Bantry Bay and the influence of the Gulf Stream made the air soft and balmy; the local flora was lush and abundant. The large Eccles Hotel had been built in the early 19th century and was popular in literary circles. One of Charlotte's heroes, Thackeray, had stayed there on his visit to Ireland and surely this must be where they stayed.

From Glengarriff it was on, eastwards to Cork, and then back to Dublin. By this time Charlotte was ready to go home. She had heard that her father was not well and she was worried. They were to arrive at the Parsonage on Tuesday, 1st August, at about 7 o'clock in the evening. 'Have things ready for tea on Tuesday evening,' she advised Martha, 'and you had better have a little cold meat or ham as well – as we shall probably get no dinner – and Mr Nicholls will want something.'[24] They arrived home safely, Arthur no longer looking like the nervous bridegroom. He had gained over twelve pounds in weight, and Charlotte was ready to take her place as mistress of the household once again.

- 8 -

Married Life

It was fortunate they were both feeling the benefit of the holiday
for Mr Brontë was indeed unwell and Arthur was immediately
called upon to take over the reins. For a month Mr Brontë took
no part in parish duties but, under Charlotte's care, he was able
to entertain Dr Burnett, the Vicar of Bradford, when he came to
preach in Haworth Church in September. Arthur made sure that
his wife had plenty to do. She was in demand continually and
found it strange after her previous quiet life. They had a stream
of visitors, including Sutcliffe Sowden and the Grants, and so
many parishioners called to wish them well that they decided to
give a tea and supper party for the staff and scholars of the
National and Sunday Schools, the choir and the bell-ringers.
Five hundred people were present – and drank Arthur's health
as a 'consistent Christian and kind gentleman'.[1]

While Charlotte was busy with domestic arrangements, she
wanted to invite Ellen, Mr and Mrs Gaskell and the Taylors to
stay with them, in turn, and see her in her new status. Arthur
too was fully occupied. Every morning he was in the National
School by 9 o'clock, giving the children religious instruction till
10.30. Most afternoons he visited the poorer parishioners and
the sick, especially those who lived at a distance. He found tasks
for his wife to do, and she was glad to help him. She felt wanted
by her husband, needed and useful, a sure combination for
happiness. In the evenings Arthur often spoke to her about her
literary work, and one night she read to him what she had
written of a new novel, *Emma,* as they sat before the fire. He
listened with care to the ten pages of the story, then said he was
afraid critics might accuse her of repetition as it again
introduced a school. 'Oh, I shall change all that,' she replied. She
had had no one to talk to, since her sisters' deaths, and it was
good to have someone to discuss her work with once more:
someone whose judgement she could rely on and whom she could
trust.

It was not her novel writing that bothered Arthur; it was her

63

letter writing. Being such a private person himself, he thought his wife wrote far too freely and rashly to her friends. The letters were in his opinion 'as dangerous as Lucifer matches'. He recommended that she ask Ellen to burn the letters as soon as she had read them; otherwise there should be no more. He dreaded their falling into the wrong hands and revealing too much of their domestic life. He insisted to Charlotte that Ellen must promise to do this or, he said, he would read every line she wrote and censor the letters himself. Charlotte suggested Ellen should write the promise on a separate piece of paper for her to give to Arthur, and enclose it with her next letter. Arthur, seeing his wife writing to Ellen just the same way as usual, persisted. Charlotte countered that, if her friend would burn the letters, they could write anything they liked to each other.[2] Arthur agreed and Ellen sent the letter in rather sarcastic terms, 'To the Revd Magister,

> My Dear Mr Nicholls – As you seem to hold in great horror the ardentia verba of feminine epistles, I pledge myself to the destruction of Charlotte's epistles henceforth, if you pledge yourself to no censorship in the matter communicated. – Yrs very truly.'

In Arthur's eyes the matter was settled, but Charlotte continued in the same style and Ellen ignored the promise she had made.[3] Arthur had never really liked Ellen very much and this episode did nothing to improve his feelings, although for Charlotte's sake he did try to hide them.

In spite of this incident Arthur and Charlotte were happy together and drawing closer. From time to time he would tell her how happy he was, and she, like any woman, was flattered and content to hear it. She felt better than she had done for some time and he was so improved that people remarked upon it and he began to worry he was putting on too much weight! He teased her about his sermons, telling her he was going to preach on some subject she disliked and then taking a quite different text, leaving her to be pleasantly disappointed. Arthur and her father were getting on well and the atmosphere in the Parsonage was harmonious.

Patrick was even recovered enough to do some preaching and Arthur felt able to undertake appointments further afield. One was an invitation to attend the consecration of the new church at Heptonstall, the old one having been damaged beyond repair in a great gale in 1847. Bishop Longley of Ripon, who had written so kindly to Arthur and Charlotte on the occasion of their marriage, was due to perform the ceremony to take place on 26th October. In the event, however, Arthur was unable to go as he had to conduct a funeral. He was not the only member of the clergy absent for, although the invitations to the laity had been sent out, most of those to the clergy had been forgotten!

On 11th November, Sir James Kay-Shuttleworth arrived at the Parsonage with a friend. He wanted to meet Arthur and see what kind of man Charlotte had married. More than that, he had had a church built at Habergham, near the gates of his home, Gawthorpe Hall and he was looking for a new incumbent; if Arthur proved acceptable, perhaps he could be persuaded to take the position. He stayed all weekend, leaving after dinner on Monday, very impressed by Arthur and making him a formal offer of the living. The stipend was £200 per annum and a new vicarage was being built. This must have been very tempting, as Arthur's income was at most £130 a year, of which only £80 was guaranteed, and the Parsonage was shared with his father-in-law. However, true to his promise to Charlotte that they would stay with her father, Arthur declined the offer, explaining his position to his would-be patron. Charlotte was gratified by his gesture which she regarded as proof of his integrity and his respect for her.

Sir James had developed a high regard for Arthur's intellect, and, before he left, asked him if he could recommend some other suitable clergyman. Arthur thought of his friend, Sutcliffe Sowden, and, but for the fact that it was pouring with rain, would have walked over straight away to Hebden Bridge to put the proposition to him; instead he wrote to him to come over the next day to discuss the pro's and con's. Such was the speed and reliability of the postal system that Sutcliffe received it in time and set off in the wind and rain on the ten-mile walk to Haworth.

Since Arthur and Charlotte's wedding, one gains the impression that they believed that matrimony would suit their friends, Sutcliffe Sowden and Ellen. On her return from honeymoon Charlotte had written to Ellen: 'I really like Mr Sowden. He asked after you. Mr Nicholls told him we expected you would be coming to stay with us in the course of three or four weeks, and he should then invite him over again as he wishes us to take sundry rather long walks, and, as he should have his wife to look after, and she was trouble enough, it would be quite necessary to have a guardian for the other lady. Mr Sowden seemed perfectly acquiescent.'[4] They had all met and, quite naturally, Sutcliffe had been paired with Ellen. If they married, it would suit both Arthur and Charlotte as they could continue their friendships at the same time, and, obtaining a good living such as Habergham with its Vicarage, Sutcliffe would want a wife. Ellen appeared a little anxious about being left on the shelf, and a clergyman would be a suitable partner for her. If Sutcliffe obtained the living at Habergham, which was not too far away, it might provide a suitable outcome for them all.

Sutcliffe discussed the proposition with Arthur and Charlotte, and Arthur arranged for him to see Sir James. Sutcliffe's only worry was that it should not become public that he was looking at another post, in case the proposition fell through. Whereupon Charlotte wrote to Ellen, 'There must be ripe consideration before he or the patron can decide. Meantime, Mr S. is most anxious that the affair should be kept absolutely quiet; in the event of disappointment it would be both painful and injurious to him if it should be rumoured in Hebden Bridge that he had thoughts of leaving. Arthur says that, if a whisper gets out, these things fly from parson to parson like wildfire.'[5]

Sutcliffe Sowden was to be disappointed, and Arthur's recommendation came to nothing. Having seen Sowden, Sir James said he could not offer him the living, using as an excuse the Bishop of Manchester. Charlotte rather smugly wrote to Ellen that Sir James says that the Bishop of Manchester stipulates clergy from his own diocese: 'Arthur says it is right and just . . . an exception would have been made in Arthur's favour but the case is not so clear with Mr Sowden. No harm will be done if the matter does not take wind, as I trust it will not.'[6]

Ellen was still enquiring in December and on 26th Charlotte wrote, 'In your last you asked about Mr Sowden and Sir James. I fear Mr Sowden has little chance of the living; he had heard nothing more of it the last time he wrote to Arthur, and in a note he had from Sir James yesterday the subject was not mentioned.'[7] Finally and rather cruelly, on 19th January, 1855: 'I fear Mr S. hardly produced a favourable impression; a strong wish was again expressed that Arthur should come but that is out of the question.'[8]

- 9 -
Charlotte's Illness and Death

Both Arthur and Charlotte enjoyed walking and taking the dogs for exercise. He was particularly fond of going up to Smith Bank (Brontë Waterfalls) and, now he was married, his wife sometimes accompanied him. An old villager remembered how Charlotte would take a board and put it across two stones and 'car down ont' green, whilst Mr Nicholls and me were wading up and down t'stream.'[1] Arthur and Charlotte were having fun together like a couple of children.

One morning in late November, Charlotte was just about to start a letter to Ellen when she was interrupted by Arthur, who suggested they go for a walk: 'We set off not intending to go far, but, though wild and cloudy, it was fair in the morning. When we had gone about half a mile on the moors, Arthur suggested the idea of the waterfall; after the melted snow, he said, it would be fine. I had often wanted to see it in its winter power, so we walked on. It was fine indeed, a perfect torrent raving over the rocks white and bountiful. It began to rain while we were watching it and we returned home under a streaming sky; however, I enjoyed the walk inexpressibly and would not have missed the spectacle on any account.'[2] Although she changed out of her wet clothes immediately upon reaching home, she felt chilled and that night had a sore throat and a cold. A week later she was feeling better but still not quite well.

Charlotte had arranged with Ellen that she would visit Brookroyd sometime in December. Ellen's sister, Mercy, was quite ill at this time. Charlotte believed this was low fever but was still prepared to go; Arthur, who was concerned to protect her delicate health and aware that Charlotte was probably pregnant, would not hear of it and insisted the visit be postponed. His caution was born out when Miss Wooler wrote to advise Charlotte that Ellen's sister was suffering from typhoid. Accordingly she wrote to Ellen saying she would not be coming for the time being, placing the blame on Arthur's authoritarian attitude and the fact that she had not quite recovered from her

67

cold: 'I shall not get leave to go to Brookroyd before Christmas now, so do not expect me. For my own part I really should have no fear and, if it just depended on me, I should come; but these matters are not quite in my power now, another must be consulted, and where his wish and judgement have a decided bias to a particular course, I make no stir but just to adopt it. Arthur is sorry to disappoint both you and me but it is his fixed wish that a few weeks should be allowed yet to elapse before we meet.'[3]

Her feelings for Arthur were in fact warmer than ever and in the same letter she says, 'Papa continues pretty well, I am happy to say, and my dear boy flourishes.' Her 'dear boy' was in fact very busy. Mr Brontë had arranged a meeting to alleviate the suffering of widows, orphans and the wounded of the battle of Sebastapol and he needed pamphlets to advertise the event but his eyesight was so poor he delegated the task to Arthur. He, in turn, requested Charlotte's help and they worked on them together. At Christmas they went their rounds of the sick and poor of the parish taking gifts of cake. In her Christmas greeting to Ellen Charlotte wrote, 'Arthur joins me in sincere good wishes for a happy Christmas and many of them to you and yours. He is well – thank God – and so am I – and he is "my dear boy" certainly – dearer now than he was six months ago – in three days we shall actually have been married that length of time!'[4]

At the beginning of January, 1855, the Nicholls received an invitation to visit Gawthorpe Hall, ostensibly so that Sir James Kay-Shuttleworth could again try to persuade Arthur to take up the living at Habergham but also to obtain Charlotte's comments on a novel he had written. The weather was wet and cold but, nevertheless, Charlotte went out walking in her thin house shoes, perhaps to escape the attention of her host, who insisted on reading aloud passages of his book. As was only to be expected with Charlotte, she caught a bad cold. On their return to Haworth they were delighted by a visit from James Adamson Bell, Arthur's cousin from Banagher and the current headmaster of the Royal Free School. With his gentlemanly manners and erudite conversation he made a great impression, and even though Charlotte was not feeling well she managed to keep going until his return to Ireland.

However, as soon as he had gone she told Ellen how she was. The symptoms she described were more akin to pregnancy than to a chill: 'My health has been really good ever since my return from Ireland till about ten days ago, when my stomach seemed to lose its tone – indigestion and continued faint sickness have been my portion ever since.'[5] A good description of morning sickness! Unfortunately, instead of improving, she became much worse. Arthur was very worried. Without her permission he sent for Dr McTurk from Bradford. He came on 30th January, confirmed the pregnancy and told Arthur that her illness would be of some duration but was not life threatening, seeing that it stemmed from natural causes. Arthur, himself, wrote to Ellen to tell her what was happening, and explaining that Charlotte had had to take to her bed. A fortnight later he wrote to Ellen again saying that his wife was 'completely prostrated with weakness and sickness and frequent fever'.[6] In desperation Charlotte penned a note to Amelia Taylor, who had had a child herself a few years earlier, 'Dear Amelia – let me speak the plain truth – my sufferings are very great – my nights indescribable – sickness with scarce a reprieve – I strain until what I vomit is mixed with blood. Medicine I have quite discontinued. If you can send me anything that will do good – do. As to my husband – my heart is knit to him – he is so tender, so good, helpful and patient.'[7] Arthur was desperately worried – she could not eat or drink and was wasting away before his eyes.

To make matters worse their old servant, Tabby, fell ill. The burden of nursing in the Parsonage was too much and Tabby was taken to her sister's home to be cared for. On the day Tabby died, 17th February, Charlotte made her will. In the greatest compliment she could pay to Arthur she left him her whole estate in the event of her death without issue.[8]

In weak handwriting, scribbled in pencil, to her friends she described Arthur's care of her. 'No kinder, better husband than mine, it seems to me, can there be in the world. I do not want now for kind companionship in health and the tenderest nursing in sickness,' she wrote to Laetitia Wheelwright.[9] To Ellen, 'I am not going to talk about my sufferings, it would be useless and painful – I want to give you an assurance which I know will comfort you – and that is I find in my husband the tenderest nurse, the kindest support – the best earthly comfort woman had, His patience never fails and it is tried by sad days and broken nights.'[10] She desperately wanted Ellen and Arthur to be friends. With resignation she wrote to Amelia Taylor, 'I would not let Arthur write to Dr Hemingway – I know it would be wholly useless.'

As well as looking after Charlotte, Arthur, no longer hale and hearty, had his duties to perform but received no help from Patrick who was suffering from bronchitis. It was Arthur who had the sad task of conducting the funeral for Tabby, while his own wife's life seemed to be moving inexorably towards its end. His feelings as he conducted the service must have been indescribable. Martha Brown, watching his care and love for his wife, became as devoted to Arthur as she once was hostile. She and her sister Tabitha tried to get Charlotte to look forward to the birth but by this time she was too weak and emaciated. She replied 'I dare say I shall be glad someday; but I am so ill, so weary.' The servants compared her to a little bird, a throssel *(sic)*, opening its beak for food. Her hand, when held up, was quite transparent.[11]By the second week in March she could no longer hold a pencil or hardly speak. Then to Arthur's great relief, she seemed to rally. She wanted food and drink and ate eagerly. It seemed there was hope for improvement. Unfortunately it did not last and she had a relapse.

Thoroughly exhausted by this time, Arthur called upon his friend, Joseph Grant, for help. Grant took over the parish work and Arthur remained at his wife's bedside as she lay there semi-conscious. At one time she opened her eyes and, seeing Arthur praying at her bedside for her recovery, she whispered, 'I am not going to die, am I ? He will not separate us, we have been so happy.'[12] On the 30th Patrick wrote to Ellen, 'We are all in great trouble, and Mr Nicholls so much that he is not sufficiently strong and composed as to be able to write. I therefore devote a few moments to tell you that my daughter is very ill, and apparently on the verge of the grave . . .' He asked her to pass the information to Miss Wooler and Amelia Taylor.

In the early hours of Saturday, 31st March, 1855, Charlotte Nicholls died. She would have been 39 in three weeks time. She and Arthur had been married for just nine months. Arthur broke down completely in a paroxysm of grief. Old Mr Brontë appeared stoical and dry-eyed but later, when Tabitha, Martha's sister, thinking he had gone into his study, opened his bedroom door, Patrick was kneeling by his bed crying, 'My poor Charlotte! My dear Charlotte!' Later she admitted she had never understood Mr Brontë before, but understood him better then.[13]

The two men did not have much time to grieve in private. As is the case with most deaths, practical details had to be attended to, letters written, arrangements made. Arthur composed himself sufficiently to write to Ellen, 'Mr Brontë's letter would prepare you for the sad intelligence I have to communicate. Our dear Charlotte is no more. She died last night of exhaustion. For the last two or three weeks we had become very uneasy about her but it was not until Sunday evening that it became apparent that her sojourn with us was likely to be short. We intend to bury her Wednesday morning.'[14] Before she had had time to receive his letter she arrived at Haworth, having left home as soon as she had received Patrick's earlier note. Through Martha he invited Ellen to stay until after the funeral. Martha took her upstairs to see the body of her dead friend and invited her to perform the funeral rites which were the custom of many rural areas. This took the form of spreading flowers and foliage over the body before the closing of the coffin. Ellen remembered the incident vividly, 'Her maid Martha brought me a tray full of evergreens and such flowers as she could procure to place on the lifeless form – my first feeling was, no, I cannot, cannot do it – next I was grateful to the maid for giving me the tender office – what made it impossible at first was the rushing recollection of the flowers I spread in her honour at her wedding breakfast and how she admired the disposal brought by Martha from the village gardens.'[15] While Ellen was performing this ceremony, Arthur and his father-in-law were busy writing the numerous letters to friends to acquaint them with the sad news, although Arthur found time once more to speak to Ellen about Charlotte's letters. He demanded that she would not show to others any letters she might have and that, on her return to Brookroyd, she would destroy them.[16] In the circumstances she could not refuse, but again broke her promise.

The funeral took place as planned on Wednesday, 4th April . The cortège consisted of Arthur and Mr Brontë, Martha and Tabitha Brown, Ellen Nussey and Margaret Wooler, Nancy Wainwright (née Garrs), who had looked after the Brontë children when young, and John Brown and his wife. Behind them came one member of almost every family in Haworth.[17] The funeral procession was the largest ever seen in the village. Sutcliffe Sowden conducted the service in a packed church. The family vault had been opened yet again and Arthur saw his wife and unborn child interred, his dreams of a happy family life buried with them. Ellen left Haworth as soon as possible after the funeral, feeling bitter against the two men for not letting her visit Charlotte earlier, and they were left to their mourning.

Although Charlotte's death certificate gave 'phthisis' (consumption) as the cause of death, there is still much controversy over this diagnosis due to the complications caused by pregnancy.[18] Whatever it was, it was no consolation to Arthur, who, dutiful as ever, felt bound by his promise to care for Mr Brontë for her sake. The funeral sermon was preached the following Sunday by Dr Cartman, Patrick's old friend from Skipton. His text was taken from Luke, chap.8 v.52, 'And all wept and bewailed her; but He said, "weep not, She is not dead, but sleepeth." ' Sutcliffe Sowden and Rev. J. H. Mitchell of Cullingworth helped out in the parish for the next week to give the two distressed men some time to regain their composure before returning to their tasks.

Cuba House – taken in the 1930s.
The caravan and figures give some idea of scale.

Photograph: Miss Valerie Landon

Margaret with Miss Valerie Landon.

Photograph: Robert Cochrane

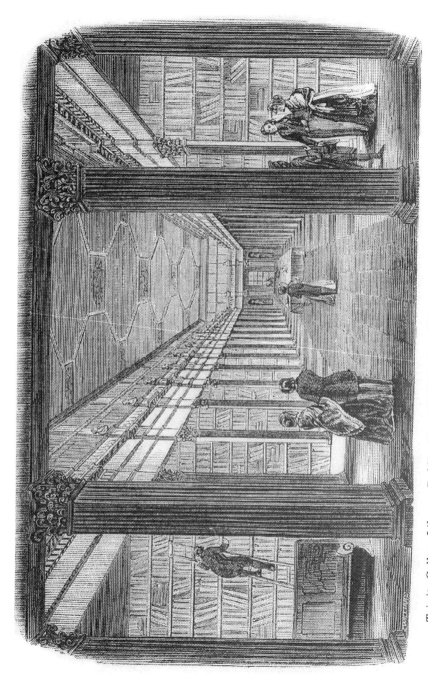

Trinity College Library, Dublin. From W. B. Taylor's History of the University of Dublin (London 1845).

The Parsonage, Haworth, as it appreared in Arthur's time.
Courtesy of the Brontë Society

The Sunday School and Sexton's House, Haworth.
Courtesy of the Brontë Society

Rev. Patrick Branwell Brontë.

Courtesy of the Brontë Society

Charlotte Brontë
from the portrait by George Richmond.
Courtesy of the Brontë Society

The Departure: second class, *by Abraham Solomon, 1855.*

Science and Society Picture Library

Beddgellert showing Royal Goat Hotel, centre left.
Lithograph by J. Newman & Co.

Mary Anna Nicholls née Bell, Arthur's second wife.
Courtesy of the Brontë Society

The Hill House, Banagher. Arthur's extension on the left.
Courtesy of the Brontë Society

The Hill House as it is today, Banagher.
Courtesy of the Brontë Society

Martha Brown.
The Brontë's servant who came to Ireland with Arthur.
Courtesy of the Brontë Society

Ellen Nussey
Charlotte's friend since their schooldays.
Courtesy of the Brontë Society

Clement K. Shorter
Editor of Illustrated London News, Tatler and Sphere.
Courtesy of the Brontë Society

Arthur walking in Banagher.
Courtesy of the Brontë Society

Arthur in later life.
Courtesy of the Brontë Society

The Bell family graves, St. Paul's Churchyard, Banagher.

Photograph: Robert Cochrane

- 10 -
Life with Patrick: Mrs. Gaskell's *Life*

The news of Charlotte's death had by now reached the London and local newspapers. Harriet Martineau, informed of Charlotte's death by John Greenwood, the Haworth stationer, wrote an obituary for the *Daily News* which was fulsome and dramatic. She described her as living 'in those dreary wilds, where she was not strong enough to roam the hills, in that retreat where her studious father rarely broke the silence – and there was no one else to do it; in that forlorn house, planted on the very clay of the churchyard; where the graves of her sisters were before her window; in such a living sepulchre her mind could not but prey on itself'[1]: strong stuff indeed and mostly inaccurate. Just the kind of story other papers and magazines could take up and elaborate upon. This they did with a vengeance, picking out and exaggerating whatever could be sensationalised. Arthur hated it and tried to take no notice but it soon became evident that it was not going to stop. He went through Charlotte's papers and discovered the facts of James Taylor's proposal, about which he had not known. Alarmed, he wondered who else knew. He wrote to Margaret Wooler, who replied that she had already destroyed the letter written to her on the subject and entirely agreed with Arthur's attitude.

Then, in June, Ellen wrote to Arthur drawing his attention to an article in *Sharpe's London Magazine*, containing such lies and untrue anecdotes about life at the Parsonage that Ellen felt vehemently that it must be refuted by a strong reply: 'Shall such [readers] be left to imbibe a tissue of lies and falsehoods, or shall an attempt be made to do justice to one who so highly deserved justice, whose very name those who knew her but speak with reverence and affection?'[2] She went on to suggest that they ask Mrs Gaskell, who, as an author, would be well versed in how to proceed. Unbeknown to them, the article had in fact been written by Mrs Gaskell herself, augmenting her knowledge of Charlotte with information and gossip gleaned from Lady Kay-

86

Shuttleworth, who had taken it, second-hand, from such an unreliable source as a servant who had been dismissed by the Brontës many years earlier.[3]

Arthur obtained a copy of the article and read it aloud to his father-in-law. For the first time in many weeks Mr Brontë laughed loud and long at the description of himself. Arthur, feeling that if they kept quiet the fuss would die down, told Ellen that he thought the article was not written with malice, although there were many mistakes. He went on to say that, even if it had been 'of a less harmful character, we should not have been inclined to take any notice of it, as, by doing so, we should have given it an importance which it would not otherwise have obtained. Charlotte herself would have acted thus; and her character stands too high to be injured by the statements in a small magazine with little influence – statements which the writer prefaces with the remark that he does not vouch for their accuracy. The many laudatory notices of Charlotte and her works which appeared since her death may well make us indifferent to the detractions of a few envious or malignant persons, as there will ever be such.'[4] Arthur, while proud of her writings, loving Charlotte as he did, wanted to keep the Charlotte he knew to himself, without exposure and innuendo. He ended his letter with a heartfelt, 'We are both well in health but lonely and desolate.'

The more Patrick thought about it, the more persuaded he became that something should be done. Much against his better judgement Arthur acquiesced and gave his permission for an account of his wife's works and life to be written by Mrs Gaskell. Mr Brontë, who had become quite enthusiastic about such an account, wrote at once to Mrs Gaskell. It was 16th June, 1855, only ten weeks after Charlotte's death, when he sent Mrs Gaskell the following letter, 'My dear Madam, Finding that a great many scribblers, as well as some clever writers have published articles, in newspapers and tracts – respecting my Dear daughter Charlotte, since her death – and seeing that many things that have been stated are true, but more false – and having reason to think that some venture to write her life, who will be ill qualified for the undertaking, I can see no better plan, under these circumstances, than to apply to some established author, to write a brief account of her life – and make some remarks on her works. You seem to me to be the best qualified for doing what I wish should be done. – If therefore you will be so kind as to publish a long, or short, account of her life and works, just as you may deem expedient and proper – Mr Nicholls and I will give you such information as you may require. I should expect and request that you would affix your name, so that the work might obtain a wide circulation, and be handed down to the latest times – . Whatever profits might arise from the sale would, of course belong to you. Mr Nicholls approves of the step I had taken and, could my daughter speak from the tomb, I feel certain she would laud our choice. Give my respectful regards to Mr Gaskell and your family, and believe me, my dear Madam, Yours very respectfully and truly, P. Brontë.'[5] The die was cast and Arthur's wish to keep Charlotte's memory to himself was broken. Mrs Gaskell, who had already given much thought to the same project, gladly agreed to open the door of the Parsonage and the lives of its inmates to the world.

Mr Brontë gave her some details of his early life and the lives of his children, adding in a postscript, 'Your kind consent has given Mr Nicholls and me great pleasure – it has broken in like a ray of light on our gloomy solitude. We shall take pleasure in seeing you here, whenever you may choose – but you will see a sad change.'[6] On a hot day five weeks later Mrs Gaskell, with Katie Winkworth for company, came to the Parsonage. It proved an awkward and painful visit. She realised at once that, while Mr Brontë was eager for the work to be written, Arthur was not. In a letter to Ellen she wrote, 'His feeling was against it being written but he yielded to Mr Brontë's impetuous wish – Mr Nicholls was far more aware of the kind of particulars which people would look for and saw how they had snatched at every gossiping account of her – Mr Brontë not perceiving the full extent of the great interest in her personal history felt by strangers.'[7]

Arthur and Mr Brontë became very emotional as they spoke of Charlotte and, by the end of the interview, they were both in tears. As she left, Mr Brontë followed her out saying, 'No quailing Mrs Gaskell. No drawing back.' She added in her letter to Marianne, 'I like Mr Nicholls.' She made no comment on Patrick.

The next day Arthur wrote to Ellen Nussey asking that she would make any letters she had had from Charlotte available to Mrs Gaskell for use in the book. Perhaps he had forgotten that he had asked her to destroy them, but more likely he had a better understanding of Ellen's character than she thought. He wrote: 'The greatest difficulty seems to be in obtaining materials to show the development of Charlotte's character. For this reason, Mrs G is anxious to see any of her letters – especially those of an early date – I think I understood you to say that you had some – if so – we should feel obliged by your letting us have any that you may think proper – not for publication, but merely to give the writer an insight into her mode of thought, – of course they will be returned after a little time – I confess that the course most consonant with my own feelings would be to take no steps in the matter but I do not think it right to offer any opposition to Mr Brontë's wishes. We have the same object in view but differ in our mode of proceeding. Mr Brontë has not been very well – excitement on Sunday (our rush-bearing) and Mrs Gaskell's visit yesterday have been rather much for him.'[8]

Arthur himself had given Mrs Gaskell a small bundle of letters, mainly addressed to Emily, but one or two to her father and one to Branwell. Ellen willingly complied with his request and eventually made available to Mrs Gaskell about 300 letters. The large number must have been a great surprise to Arthur. Mrs Gaskell had felt the visit to Haworth stressful; she was somewhat in awe of Mr Brontë and getting information from Arthur, who was not enthusiastic about the idea, would not have been easy. Added to that, the two men's obvious distress and tearfulness when discussing Charlotte made it an experience she was not keen to repeat. For their part, the two clergymen had been expecting a further visit or, at the very least, some sort of progress report; instead she was travelling far and wide, interviewing and talking to anyone she could find who had had any contact with Charlotte. Together with Ellen's letters she was amassing a great deal of information.

She had visited the Parsonage in July, and six months had now elapsed. In January, 1856, thinking that she must be having difficulty due to the scarcity of material, Mr Brontë wrote to her, 'Mr Nicholls and I often think of what you have so obligingly entered on, of what the public will expect of you on whatever subject you may write, and the few facts and incidents you have of a biographical nature. We so frequently talk over and meditate on these things, that we are forced at last, to solve the difficulty by saying you must draw on the resources of your own mind.'[9]

Life was just beginning to get back to some semblance of normality in the Parsonage when Martha, exhausted, became seriously ill, as did her father, John Brown. Because of this she could not be cared for at home, and, with only men in the house, could not be properly treated at the Parsonage. She was, therefore, sent to Mrs Dran's Alms-houses in Leeds for treatment and rest. Her sister Eliza stood in for her at the Parsonage and Arthur visited her in Leeds to make sure she was comfortable and was being well looked after; Patrick offered to send her money. Shortly after her return her father died. Arthur conducted the funeral service, with Patrick and the Brown family sitting in the Brontë family pew. Martha never forgot their kindness.

A year after Mrs Gaskell's visit, Mr Gaskell had sent Mr Brontë a copy of the sermon he had preached in thanksgiving for the end of the Crimean War. Writing to thank him, Mr Brontë inquired, 'We often wonder here, how Mrs Gaskell is getting on, with her mournful but interesting task.' She was needing to see more papers and obtain more information from the Parsonage but was afraid to go on her own. The very next day after Mr Brontë had written his letter she turned up with Sir James Kay-Shuttleworth, relying on his overbearing and autocratic attitude to help her in her dealings.[10] Martha was still away, the young Eliza was the only servant in the house and Mr Brontë was ill in bed with bronchitis. Poor Arthur was overwhelmed. Sir James simply rode rough-shod over any objections, took whatever Mrs Gaskell wanted and more beside. He even persuaded Patrick to allow Charlotte's portrait to be photographed, something Arthur had objected to in the past. Mr Brontë said the last word would have to be with Arthur, but Sir James said that he knew Mr Nicholls would give permission. Mrs Gaskell would send over a photographer from Manchester so that he would not even have to part with the picture. By his high-handed manner, he and Mrs Gaskell had, in her own words, 'carried off' the manuscripts of *The Professor* and *Emma* and 'a whole heap of those minute writings', as well as permission for the photograph. The two clergymen felt they had entertained a whirlwind.

When Arthur learned that Sir James was planning to edit *The Professor* for publication he was roused to action. Knowing his late wife's opinion of Sir James' literary skill, he felt she would turn in her grave if he let this happen. Arthur informed the high-handed baronet he would do it himself, recovered the manuscript, and set about proof-reading the book. Charlotte had initially named it *The Master* but had then changed her mind. She wrote the new title on a piece of paper and stuck this over the original.[11] While he was as methodical and careful in his proof-reading as he was in everything else, Arthur altered very little. He wrote to George Smith, 'I have read *The Professor* over to Mr Brontë. Our opinion is that, with the exception of two or three strong expressions which might be open to misinterpretation, no revision of the manuscript is necessary. Indeed, if any extensive alteration had been requisite we could not have consented to the publication of the tale. We have erased the few seemingly objectionable phrases.' Mrs Gaskell, in close contact with George Smith over her biography, complained of coarseness in Charlotte's writing and said that Arthur had not altered enough. However, they did not feel they could get Arthur to change any more of his wife's words. The publisher therefore decided to delay publication until after the biography as her upbringing would have explained the reason for her coarseness and nullify any effect on the public. To modern eyes it is difficult to see what was being complained of and, considering the problems Mrs Gaskell's biography caused, she was in no position to criticise. The book was published in June, 1857, some four months after the biography, with no mention of the fact that it was he who had edited it, other than his small addition to Charlotte's preface. The reviews were rather subdued but Arthur had not expected it to be a great success and was not really disappointed. He was quite satisfied with sales of the work. He felt he had done his duty by Charlotte.

By late 1856, he had begun to be very worried that Mrs Gaskell would make too free with quotations from the letters she had seen, but which he had stipulated at the very beginning were 'not for publication but merely to be used to give the writer an insight into her mode of thought'. In spite of hinting that they would like to see the book before publication, Arthur and Patrick were never shown it, unlike Ellen, to whom it was read aloud.

Letters were quoted in long extracts throughout the book, quite contrary to Arthur's wishes and, when Mrs Gaskell discovered at this late stage that legally the copyright to the letters belonged to him, she was horrified. His ownership of the copyright, as Charlotte's heir, also applied to the many letters to Ellen; even though the letters were her property, Arthur could prohibit their publication. Without the letters, the biography would lose much of its credibility. George Smith, whose company, Smith Elder & Co. was to publish the work, suggested a rather underhand way of obtaining permission. He would send Arthur a document which he said was a 'business form of application' which would transfer the copyright 'materials of the biography' to Mrs Gaskell. They hoped Arthur would look upon this as the usual thing to be done and sign without question. They did not know their man. He replied that he must decline to sign the document, 'not because I have the slightest intention of making any pecuniary claim on Mrs Gaskell on account of the work on which she is engaged; but simply, if I did so, I should therefore be precluded from making any further use of the manuscripts referred to'.[12] He further explained that he had only agreed to help Mrs Gaskell out of deference to Mr Brontë's wishes but had never had any idea of giving up the papers, or letting her have exclusive right to them. George Smith managed to make Arthur feel guilty, implying he would be the one to blame if the biography was never published, and that he would be reneging on his implied agreement if he did not sign.

Under this pressure he eventually acquiesced but wrote to George Smith a letter which showed, not only his anger, but also his regard for Charlotte's memory which he felt was being harmed: 'I never entered into any arrangement with Mrs Gaskell to convey to her the copyright of any of my wife's manuscripts for the purpose of the memoir or any other – I trust I shall not be required to do anything more in the matter, which from the beginning has been a source of pain and annoyance to me; as I have been dragged into sanctioning a proceeding, utterly repugnant to my feelings – indeed nothing but an unwillingness to thwart Mr Brontë's wishes could have induced me to acquiesce in a project, which in my eyes is little short of desecration.'[13]

Mrs Gaskell, of course, was delighted at the outcome and pleased she had not had to deal with the fierce correspondence with Mr Nicholls. She found him 'a terribly tickle person to have to do with', and would have been put off by the first refusal.[14] Now the way was clear for her to complete her work. On 7th February, 1857, the book was ready. She was paid £800 by George Smith for the English copyright and set off immediately for Italy.

The Life of Charlotte Brontë was published on 25th March. All 2,021 copies were sold out by April. A further 1,500 were printed, followed by 700 more in May; it was a runaway success. Arthur bitterly regretted not having insisted on seeing the book before publication – he felt dismayed and humiliated by the description of his proposal to Charlotte and its sequel. He realised it could only have come from one source, Ellen, and the more he read, the deeper he found her involvement. He had tried to be conciliatory to her in his letters, had gone along with her and Mr Brontë's wish for a biography and now he felt betrayed. Even in old age he found it difficult to forgive her role in laying open the private lives of his wife and her family to public scrutiny. He wrote to George Smith that he had read the book with 'inexpressible pain – Mrs Gaskell has done justice to her subject – she has however fallen into many errors, but fewer, perhaps, than might have been expected. She has moreover inserted some things, which ought never to have been published – It was not without reason that I instinctively shrank from the proposal of a biography – but I suppose it matters not, provided the curiosity of the Public be gratified.'[15] The book was so popular that it became a subject for discussion by the newspapers, both national and local. *The Bradford Observer*, the local paper, reprinted the story of Arthur's proposal, making it available to be read by his friends and colleagues, to say nothing of his congregation and the people of Haworth. It was torture to such a sensitive and private man.

Resulting Publicity and Criticism

When Mrs Gaskell returned from Italy she found herself the centre of legal mayhem. One libel action by Lady Scott (the former Mrs Robinson) had been settled in her absence and now W. W. Carus-Wilson, the son of that William Carus-Wilson who had founded the Clergy School at Cowan Bridge, was threatening another, breathing fire over the description of his father and his school. Not only had Mrs Gaskell criticised his father's running of the school but the publication of the biography made clear that Charlotte's description of Lowood School in *Jane Eyre* was based on her experiences as a pupil there. Wilson and his supporters were furious, and circulated articles denigrating both Mrs Gaskell's and Charlotte's accounts. They sent copies of his letters to the local papers, *Daily News, Leeds Mercury* and *Halifax Guardian*[1] and distributed them by post, even sending a copy to Mr Brontë at the Parsonage. Apart from his own views, Mr Wilson included a long letter from 'the lady who was superintendent of that institution in 1824': 'In July 1824 Mr Brontë arrived at Cowan Bridge with two of his daughters, Maria and Elizabeth; the children were so delicate there were doubts whether they could be admitted into the school. They were received, and went on so well that their father brought in September two more, Charlotte and Emily. During both of these visits Mr Brontë stayed at the school, sat at the table with the pupils, and saw the whole routine of the establishment.

'They all inherited consumption from their mother and were taken home; none of them, as has been stated, had any attack of fever or died at the school. I can truly say that none of the pupils were denied a sufficient quantity of good food; they were never limited: meat, vegetables and puddings daily in abundance; any statement to the contrary is most false. Charlotte was a bright, clever, happy little girl, never in disgrace. In size remarkably diminutive, and if, has been asserted, she never grew an inch after leaving school, she must have been a literal dwarf . . . Let us hope that, in caricaturing an institution which has been such a blessing to the daughters of her own church, she had no injurious motives, but, misled by a vivid imagination, and a dim recollection of thirty years, when she was but a child, she published in an unguarded moment, unmindful of the consequences, misstatements, the tendency of which has been to calumniate a most excellent institution, and to bring disgrace on religion . . .'

Mr Wilson went on to say, 'With the above we would take the testimony of hundreds of pupils, who with their parents have gratefully acknowledged the advantages they received at these institutions, rather than the account of one, however talented, who when but a child of nine left the establishment, and has so ungenerously cast odium upon him who first planned such a help to our poorer clergy, and who has yearly undertaken the risk of the support of near 300 pupils and teachers, for, including a preparatory school, there are about 150 daughters of clergymen boarded, clothed and educated, at only £14 a year each, including everything and in the "Servants' School", above 100 girls trained for service, each paying only £10 a year.

'The schools are situated in Westmoreland, built on Mr Carus Wilson's property, half a mile from Casterton Hall, his residence. They stand amid beautiful scenery, on high and healthy situations. They require above £1,000 a year, in addition to the payments of the pupils, to cover all expenses.'

Arthur, whose normal attitude was 'least said, soonest mended', would not stand by and see Charlotte's veracity questioned and wrote supporting her view of the school:

'On Saturday last you published, by the request of Mr W. W. Carus Wilson, an extract from a review, containing, he says, "a complete answer to the statements regarding his father's charitable institutions."

'The statements referred to are, I presume, the following:- That the unhealthy situation of Cowan Bridge, unwholesome food, and exposure to cold etc., enfeebled the girls, and predisposed them to disease; that fever broke out among them; that about forty of them suffered from it; that the surgeon, who was called in , condemned the girls' daily food by the expressive action of spitting out a portion of it, which he had taken in order to taste it; that the school was removed to a new situation, and a committee of management appointed.

'Now let us examine the "complete answer", and see how these charges are disposed of. He praises the situation of the school, "on Mr Carus Wilson's property, half a mile from Casterton Hall, high and healthy"; but he has not the candour to state that this description applies to the *present* site, and *not that referred to in 'Jane Eyre'*.

He eulogises Mr Wilson's liberality, but omits to state that funds are raised from the public for the support of the establishments which Mr W.W.Carus Wilson modestly calls "his father's charitable institutions".

'He makes *no mention whatever* of the condemnation of the girls' daily food by the medical man, of the fever which scourged the school, and the consequent change of site and reformation of the establishment.

'But surely the former superintendent, "whose able letter appeared in a review," will supply the gentleman's omissions, . . . She lays before us a bill of fare at Cowan Bridge – "Meat, vegetables, and puddings, daily in abundance." Very good, madam! But what about the cooking that spoiled these provisions, boiled the puddings in unclean water, compounded the Saturday's nauseous mess from the fragments accumulated in a dirty larder during the week, and too often sent up porridge, not merely burnt, but with offensive fragments of other substances discoverable in it?'

W. Carus-Wilson, writing in refutation of Nicholls, did, however, admit that, 'During the Spring of 1825 a low fever though not an alarming one prevailed', and, in countering criticisms of the food, agreed that the doctor did speak 'rather scornfully of one dish – rice pudding, but as the ingredients were rice, sugar and milk, its effects could hardly have been as serious as have been affirmed' and said 'thoughtless servants will spoil food even in private families'.

This was the beginning of three months of accusations and denials with the correspondence becoming ever more bitter and angry. To prove that it was not just Charlotte, Arthur quoted from a letter received from another pupil, 'I attribute my illness to the unhealthy situation of the school, the long walks in bad weather (for in winter our feet were often wet during the whole of the service), and scanty and ill-prepared food . . . The housekeeper was very dirty with the cooking. I have frequently seen grease swimming on the milk and water we had for breakfast in consequence of its having been boiled in a greasy copper, and I perfectly well remember once being sent for a cup of tea for a teacher, who was ill in bed, and no spoon being to hand, the housekeeper stirred it with her finger, she being engaged in cutting up raw meat at the time. I could give you scores of such instances as these which fell under my own observation. Our food was almost always badly cooked, and besides that we certainly had not enough of it, whatever may be said to the contrary . . .'

Wilson had also written to *The Times* and, when they did not print Arthur's reply, Patrick Brontë, in the absence of Arthur in Ireland, wrote to George Smith asking him to have the letter published in *The Times* as an advertisement. However, George Smith prevailed upon Patrick not to pursue this course. When Arthur returned, the correspondence was being carried on by Sarah Baldwin, a former pupil at Cowan Bridge. She had not been a contemporary of the Brontë girls and some improvement had taken place at the School after they had left. Although Arthur pointed this out, she continued to defend Wilson and the School in long and forceful letters to the *Halifax Guardian*. The whole situation was getting out of hand and the editor decided to intervene. He wrote to Mr Brontë asking him if he might drop the publication of correspondence on the subject. This was agreed but, even so, Sarah Baldwin, refusing to submit to the closing of the correspondence, sent in another letter to be published as an advertisement, to which Arthur was allowed to reply. He wrote a final letter, again pointing out that Sarah Baldwin could not know what conditions were like as she was not there until after the Brontë girls had left. He ended, 'I have discharged a painful if necessary duty. – Henceforth Charlotte Brontë's assailants may growl and snarl over her grave undisturbed by me.'

Although this particular correspondence had ended, rumblings in other quarters went on, from William Dearden jumping to Patrick's defence, to Harriet Martineau almost hysterical in her accusation that Charlotte's statements about her were not true.[2] Arthur and Patrick spent much time writing soothing and conciliatory letters but finally withdrew from any further public involvement. When Miss Martineau asked for the return of her letters to Charlotte Arthur immediately complied. He wrote, 'with the exception of two or three referring to her misunderstanding with Miss Brontë, I have read none of them, I have merely taken them out of their covers in order to remove any memoranda enclosed with them by my wife.' Miss Martineau had had it from John Greenwood that the letters had been burnt; Arthur continued, 'His position is not such as would have enabled him to know anything of Miss Brontë's affairs further than what he learned by gossiping with servants. His relation to Miss Brontë consisted being the recipient of her bounty and advice when in distress from the claims of a large family.'[3] In response to a further query he agreed that he had told Mrs Gaskell that he had burnt 'all C.B.'s letters to himself,' but had given a packet of her papers to Mrs Gaskell.

With the publication of *The Life of Charlotte Brontë* the trickle of literary tourists finding their way to Haworth became a stream, much to Arthur's alarm. He felt his privacy was being invaded by people peering round the Parsonage and the church, looking for souvenirs and seeking information from the local inhabitants. The inns increased their prices, the shopkeepers experienced an upsurge in trade, and Brontë memorabilia were eagerly sought – Brontëmania had set in. The Duke of Devonshire visited the Parsonage and stayed for an hour. He was greatly impressed and later sent a large present of game in gratitude and invited both Arthur and Patrick to Bolton Abbey. There were many visits and letters from old friends and colleagues and all of this helped Arthur to fill the void left by Charlotte's death.

The first furore gradually died down, but life in the Parsonage would never be the same again. Before very long, letters were being received from complete strangers, some requesting samples of Charlotte's handwriting. Much to Arthur's disapproval, Patrick, who enjoyed the vicarious fame, took to cutting up some of Charlotte's old letters into strips or small squares and sending them out to the supplicants to satisfy this demand. From far and wide, admirers of Charlotte's work requested a visit to the Parsonage. Although Arthur and Patrick were of such different temperaments, they each in their own way wanted to do the best they could for Charlotte's memory and received visitors with courtesy and charm. Most were surprised to find that Mrs Gaskell's picture of Haworth and its clergymen was, to say the least, exaggerated. James Hoppin, an American professor from Yale, enjoyed a talk with Patrick; Jarvis Raymond, editor of the *New York Times*, was welcomed and he told the two men that he found Mrs Gaskell's description 'too sombre and repulsive'. Arthur and Patrick smiled at each other and Mr Brontë answered, 'Well, I think Mrs Gaskell tried to make us all appear as bad as she could.' Another visitor was the Rev. Edward White Benson a future Archbishop of Canterbury. More locally, a correspondent from the *Bradford Observer* called and wrote an article refuting some of Mrs Gaskell's wilder colouring.

The next year, 1858, Patrick had a new memorial tablet to his family made to replace the existing one as it was not large enough to hold all the family names; indeed Charlotte's name had had to be placed on a separate tablet. When the old one had been taken down, Arthur was anxious that it should not get into the wrong hands, broken up and parts sold as souvenirs. He ordered the Sexton, William Brown, to smash it with a hammer into small pieces and bury them four feet deep in the Parsonage garden. He stood over the Sexton while he did this to ensure its safe disposal.

A bad attack of bronchitis that year left the old man very frail and he was now dependent on his curate to perform almost all of the parish duties. Arthur conducted all three services each Sunday, although Mr Brontë, when fit enough, preached one of the sermons, usually in the afternoon. It was now as much as he could do to walk slowly round the garden. If Arthur were out, Patrick would leave his newspaper on the table, with a message to Martha written across it to tell her he was only out in the garden if she wanted him.

Following their agreement for the publication of *The Professor*, Arthur, until he left Haworth, was in regular correspondence with George Smith. He was pleased with the way the publisher had agreed not to make alterations to the book, as he knew that Charlotte had taken a strong line over this with her previous two books. Although the publishing of Mrs Gaskell's *Life* caused some problems for the relationship, these were quickly dispelled when *The Professor* came out some months later. The letters had a friendly tone and Arthur always gave news of Mr Brontë with affection.

The Life of Charlotte Brontë had sold so well that a new cheaper edition was to be produced. At the same time Mrs Gaskell had heard that George Smith was to bring out a new literary publication, *The Cornhill Magazine*. She suggested that he might approach Arthur to allow him to include the chapters of Charlotte's last unfinished work, *Emma*. She pointed out that if he did this she could then include these fragments at the end of her book and it would be a further inducement to sales. George

Smith replied that she could ask Arthur herself but she said that she was too afraid to do so. This seems largely the result of a guilty conscience over the way she had treated Arthur, together with a preference for someone else to do the dirty work. After her first visit to discuss the autobiography, when Arthur had reluctantly agreed to participate she had written, 'I like Mr Nicholls'; the second meeting she had gone in with the overbearing Sir James Kay-Shuttleworth and, on publication, had left George Smith to deal with Arthur's anger and hurt.

The publisher did agree to make an approach without mentioning her name. Arthur was delighted at the suggestion, especially at the proposal that Thackeray should be asked to write an introduction to the piece, for he knew how much Charlotte had admired him. He copied the manuscript, described how he and Charlotte had read the chapters together, and even volunteered that Smith might be interested in some of the poems by Branwell, Emily and Anne. A few days later he went so far as to send the original manuscript, with the proviso that it be returned. When after several weeks and an anxious letter of enquiry it arrived, he wrote acknowledging its safe return, 'I prize it very much as the last thing of the kind written by the Author.'

The first number of the *Cornhill Magazine* came out in December, 1859, and George Smith sent Arthur and Patrick a copy. Arthur responded that they found the contents 'most gratifying'. Mr Brontë had taken particular pleasure in an article on the Volunteers (a cross between the T.A. and the Home Guard) as he had been a member himself at the time of the Napoleonic wars, 50 years previously, and still maintained a keen interest in their doings. Arthur had read it to the old man reviving happy memories of his youth. Arthur had always had an interest in nature and had taken to studying specimens under a microscope, a scientific interest popular at that time, and he had read the article, *Studies of Animal Life,* with 'pleasure and profit'.[4] When the article on *Emma* did not immediately appear Arthur was worried, but George Smith reassured him and, when, in March, 1860, the article and fulsome introduction appeared in print, Arthur commented, 'Mr Thackeray's introductory remarks to *The Last Sketch* are greatly admired in this neighbourhood, and for my own part I feel deeply indebted for them.' Arthur and Patrick were further delighted to receive a personal letter from Thackeray, who had been Charlotte's hero and was one of the literary giants of the day. In later editions of the magazine two poems by Charlotte and one by Emily were published. Arthur was in favour of this type of publication, proud and eager to show his wife's skills but against prurient personal details being disclosed.

By now Patrick could no longer walk down to the church; the last occasion on which he had preached a sermon was 30th October, 1859, and by August, 1860, he was confined to his bed.[5] This threw a further burden of work on Arthur as, in addition to his concern for the parish, he had to supervise and help with the care of his father-in-law. There had been no Confirmation Service in Haworth since the See of Ripon was formed in 1836, indeed not since 1824. The Bishop of Ripon, Dr Longley, arranged that he would come and carry out the ceremony at Haworth on 6th August. It seems strange that this should happen after so long a gap but that year, 1860, Dr Longley was translated to the Archbishopric of York and it was probable that he was taking his last opportunity to visit Haworth before he left Ripon. Arthur would have had to ensure that each candidate knew his catechism and had been baptised. The day before the Confirmation he baptised 13 people in a mass service.[6] Arthur also had to play host and entertain the Bishop at the Parsonage. Before Dr Longley left, true to his kindly nature, he visited his old colleague in his bedroom, giving rise to speculation that Patrick was actually dying. The rumour spread to one newspaper in the area, which, in covering the story, declared it was likely that Arthur would be the next incumbent at Haworth. He was extremely angry at reading this, and the implication that he was just waiting for the old man to die. Whilst in his heart he no doubt wished to succeed to Haworth, his very proper nature felt it unbecoming and insensitive to express such sentiments whilst the present incumbent was still alive and he wrote to the paper saying he had no expectation of obtaining the appointment.[7]

Later that year, Richard Monckton Milnes, who had visited Arthur at Kirk Smeaton, called at the Parsonage with a request to see some of Branwell's papers. He also visited William Brown to see some of Branwell's letters to his brother, John Brown, the former Sexton and Branwell's friend. Arthur and Mr Brontë were reluctant to publish these papers because of the nature of the contents, which could perhaps have referred to Branwell's affair with Mrs Robinson and they discussed with Monckton Milnes their decision not to publish. After the visit Arthur wrote to him, 'Neither Mr Brontë or I have any intention of publishing them; indeed we had some time ago already refused to allow them to be printed; for leaving their merit as literary compositions out of the question altogether, we saw plainly that their subject could not fail to give pain to some persons – We are therefore glad to find that your opinion fully demonstrates the propriety of our decision.'[8]

Monckton Milnes had most likely heard of these letters from Mrs Gaskell, who had become aware of them when writing her biography. His interest was probably in the more salacious parts of the letters as he was known in literary circles for his collection of dubious materials. One can only think that Monckton Milnes conducted the discussion on propriety tongue-in-cheek!

On 2nd October, 1860, Patrick Brontë wrote a short note to Mrs Gaskell saying he would be glad to see her if she would call. She was very wary about making another visit, but was persuaded to do so by her daughter, Meta. She accompanied her mother for moral support and on October 25th they arrived at the Parsonage to find the old man confined to his bed. They had a long chat until it was almost time for Arthur to return from school: then Mr Brontë hinted that they had better take their leave. It seems fairly obvious that he would want them to go to avoid any confrontation between Mrs Gaskell and Arthur, whom he knew were anathema to each other. She took his hints as an indication that Mr Brontë was as terrified of his son-in-law as by now she had convinced herself that she was. Even so, this did not prevent her from making disparaging remarks about Patrick following her visit.

Whilst in Haworth she took the opportunity to visit another of her sources in the district, the Greenwood family. They had disliked Arthur because he had not supported their plans to reproduce memorabilia. Subsequently they felt they had further cause for complaint and Mrs Greenwood poured out this story to Mrs Gaskell: when they had told Mr Nicholls they wished their youngest son to be christened 'Brontë', he had, in Mr Brontë's hearing, flatly refused to do so. They, the Greenwoods, had therefore left the child unbaptised. When he was several months old, he became ill and they were fearful he would not survive. Upon hearing of this Mr Brontë sent for them and christened the child in his bedroom. He entered this in the Baptismal Register himself, '14th November 1859 – Brontë Greenwood'. When Arthur needed the Register for the next baptism he saw what

Patrick had done. The Greenwoods alleged that he went straight up to the Parsonage and into the bedroom and stormed, 'So I see you have christened your namesake!' and the only way for Patrick to calm him was to explain that he had done it to prevent Arthur being in trouble if the child had died unbaptised. This story was quoted by Mrs Gaskell and her supporters as proof that Arthur was widely disliked in the village.

It is easy to understand Arthur's reluctance to christen the child Brontë, and certainly Patrick did perform the ceremony, but one wonders how Mrs Greenwood was able to give so graphic a picture of what went on in the Parsonage between the two men. While at the Greenwoods Mrs Gaskell also met William Brown who is reputed to have said, 'Mr Nicholls and Mr Brontë still live together, ever near, but ever separate.'

Meta, in an account of their visit, wrote to a friend that this was, 'a specimen of Mr N's sullen, obstinate rooted objection to any reverence being paid to Miss B. One might almost say at any rate to people caring to remember her as an authoress.' – this from someone who had never even met Nicholls. Another from Mrs Gaskell, 'He is more unpopular in the village than ever; and seems to have even a greater aversion than formerly to any strangers visiting his wife's grave; or indeed to any reverence paid to her memory, even by those who knew her and loved her for her own sake.'[9]

Arthur's enthusiasm for the publication of Charlotte's works and the reception received by many visitors to the Parsonage, who found him and Mr Brontë courteous and welcoming, would appear to give the lie to this story. The trouble between Arthur and the Greenwoods was due to their attempts to profit by their association with Charlotte – she bought her paper from John Greenwood. Mrs Gaskell's information on Haworth and Arthur's character came mainly from Ellen Nussey, who was jealous of Arthur usurping her position with Charlotte, and the Greenwoods. Having recognised Arthur's reserve at their meeting to discuss the biography, she had flouted his wishes and published details which were hurtful to him. Because of this she dare not go back to talk to him further and this led her to accept anything derogatory she heard from comparatively few people. If she had collaborated more with Arthur, the biography would probably have been more accurate and circumspect, but less sensational and less successful, and perhaps the Brontës would not have become as famous as they are today.

Patrick's Death; Leaving Haworth

On 20th June, 1855 Rev. Patrick Brontë had made his will. He left £40 to be divided between his brothers and sisters by his brother Hugh, £30 to Martha for her long and faithful service, and the remainder of his estate to, 'my beloved and esteemed Son-in Law, the Rev. Arthur Bell Nicholls, B.A.' Arthur was to be the sole executor and the document was witnessed by Joseph Redman and Eliza Brown.[1] This surely points to the fact that the two men were getting along well together after Charlotte's death; Patrick could easily have distributed his possessions differently, with no advantage to Arthur, if he had wanted. When Patrick died in 1861 at the age of 84, his death certificate recorded: 'Chronic bronchitis; dyspepsia; convulsions, duration 9 hours.' Arthur and Martha were with him at the end. He had been the incumbent of Haworth for 41 years. Ellen Nussey, away in the Isle of Wight, wrote to Arthur to enquire how Patrick had died, but Arthur sent only the tersest of replies, 'Dear Madam, I have little information to communicate on the subject of your note. Mr Brontë had been confined to his bed for several months. On Friday morning (June 7, 1861) he was seized with convulsions and died in the course of the afternoon. I am dear madam, Yours very truly, A. B. Nicholls.'

Arthur made all the arrangements in accordance with Patrick's wish that his funeral was to be simple. He had, like the Heatons earlier, applied to the Secretary of State for permission for the body of his father-in-law to be placed in the family vault. There was to be no tolling of the funeral bell, no psalms were to be sung and the service was to be plain and dignified. News of his death had quickly spread and when, just before noon on 12th June, the cortège left the Parsonage, the church was completely full. Many could not find a pew and stood in every available space. Outside in the churchyard and along the lane, hundreds more stood in silence. All the shops in Haworth closed as a mark of affection and respect.

The service was conducted by the Vicar of Bradford, Dr

Burnett, assisted by William Cartman. The coffin was carried into church by six of Patrick's colleagues and was followed by Arthur, Martha and Eliza Brown and their mother and Nancy Wainwright (née Garrs). Behind them came the church Trustees. During the proceedings Arthur was so distressed he had to be supported by William Cartman. He had lost his last link with Charlotte, it was almost too much to bear, and he returned desperately upset to the Parsonage.

He did not know that on that very day the church Trustees held a meeting to decide the appointment of a new incumbent. Only after they had convened, was it thought that perhaps it was in rather bad taste, having just returned from the funeral. The meeting was adjourned and not reconvened for several months.

Arthur returned to his parish duties after a few days and was able to read the prayers at the traditional Sunday memorial service on 23rd June. Again the service was conducted by Dr Burnett and again the church was full. It seemed to most people in Haworth a foregone conclusion that Arthur would take his father-in law's place. In the Haworth Parish Register he was signing himself, 'Officiating Minister'. For the next two months all seemed to be running smoothly when he was faced with another personal tragedy: his best friend, Sutcliffe Sowden, was drowned.

He had been taken ill returning from visiting a parishioner on the dark, stormy night of 8th August and had fallen into the canal at Hebden Bridge. Arthur was asked to conduct the funeral service, a duty which must have been terribly hard for him coming so soon after the loss of his father-in-law. Seeing the shops and mills closed and silent, seeing the quiet crowds lining the streets and the village children carrying flowers to lay on the grave were great reminders of the events in Haworth two months previously. When he read the words of the service he was at times inaudible. He later wrote, 'It was hard to read the Service over one whose intimate friendship I have enjoyed for so many years and whom I have looked on as more of a relation than a friend. Indeed I have no relations whose loss I would deplore more sincerely.'[2]

Back in Haworth Arthur's position was not as cut and dried as he and most of the other people in Haworth had felt it to be. The Trustees held another meeting. Two of the 12 did not attend and one of those present was a Dissenter. Arthur was proposed as the next incumbent. A vote was taken and four, including the chairman, Richard Heaton, voted for him; five were against and the Dissenter abstained. Arthur had lost. Discussions were held with Dr Burnett, who put up another candidate, Rev. John Wade. At a third and final meeting Wade was voted incumbent by seven votes to five. Arthur's position was now untenable; he could not remain as assistant curate when the Trustees had shown such lack of faith in him. Immediately on being informed of their discussion on September 18th he handed in his resignation.

As if he had not lost enough, he now had no home and no job. The decision was a shock to the people of Haworth. To all intents and purposes he had been the incumbent in all but name for the last five years. One villager, reminiscing in later life, remarked, 'He (Arthur) ought to ha' had Haworth Church. I never thought but he would ha' had it and he did himself. All t'church folks wanted him to have it and he would ha had it but for one o' t'trustees, a girt manufacturer and a Methody, and he'd casting vote – it came to an odd un. They wanted him to come back and preach once for rish bearing Sunday, but he wouldn't. He thought he'd gotten out of t'church and he'd never have to face Haworth again.'[3]

Why, after all these years of faithful service, he was not given the incumbency we can only speculate. After Charlotte had died there was an article in the paper saying that Dr Burnett had promised the living to Arthur if he stayed with Mr Brontë. This was subsequently shown to be a complete fabrication and withdrawn, but mud sticks, and the Trustees were notorious for not being pushed. Another reason given was that he had upset the Heaton family some years earlier and it was still held against him.

When Michael Heaton of Ponden Hall had died in 1856, his eldest son Richard had asked Arthur if he could bury him in the family grave. Arthur had said he could not, as that part of the graveyard had been closed. The Heatons had then written to the Secretary of State and obtained permission to open the grave and Mr Grant had conducted the funeral. Much has been made of this incident, which has been cited as an example of Arthur's high-handedness, a cause for dislike in the parish and one of the reasons for the rejection, by the Trustees, of his candidature for the incumbency on Mr Brontë's death.

This is totally misleading. Arthur had no power to re-open a grave in the closed part of the churchyard. The only person who could allow this was the Secretary of State. It was not unusual for these applications to be made by the family of the deceased and, indeed, the procedure was so common that the reply saying that a licence would be sent to the incumbent granting permission was on a printed form (albeit in copperplate script) with only gaps for the details to be filled in.[4] Arthur would surely have known this, and most likely would have advised the Heatons where to write. With regard to Grant conducting the funeral, this again was not significant as, from time to time, he conducted burials (and weddings and baptisms) when Arthur or Mr Brontë had other engagements. As for the Trustees' vote which lost Arthur the curacy, Richard Heaton was, in fact, one of the Trustees who voted for him.

There were other possible reasons. Arthur was known to be High Church and very much against Dissenters; one of the trustees, a powerful manufacturer, was a Methodist; not everybody was happy with the notoriety brought to the town following Charlotte's death, and some wanted a break from the Brontës. Perhaps they thought a new incumbent would put an end to all this. In Wade's favour, he was a much younger man, 25 to Arthur's 42. He was married, and a wife was always a useful adjunct for a clergyman; Arthur had not shown any inclination to re-marry. Perhaps what counted most of all: Wade had a private income. The Trustees could leave him to look after the well-being of the Parsonage without bothering them for more money. Perhaps, in accordance with tradition, the Haworth Trustees wanted to assert their independence. Whatever the reasons for their decision, Arthur was left disillusioned and deeply hurt.

There was little time, however, for self-pity; the practicalities had to be faced. The Parsonage had to be cleared for the new incumbent as soon as possible and Arthur had to decide where he was going to live. He selected the items he wished to keep and then employed a local auctioneer, John Cragg of Keighley, to take an inventory and arrange a quick sale as Wade was anxious to take over. Only four days after Arthur resigned Wade had taken his first service. Arthur had no wish to linger where he was not wanted and he decided to return to Ireland to his Aunt's home as soon as the house was cleared.

Before the inventory was made he gave many items away to Martha and Tabitha, her sister. Charlotte and Emily's black wood travelling trunk which was bought by the sisters when they were in Brussels was given to Tabitha, who liked the blue

107

flowered paper with which it was lined. He also gave her Anne's writing desk and a dress of Charlotte's which she altered to fit her daughter. The blue and white china toilet set which had stood for so long in Patrick's bedroom he passed on to his former landlady. Martha already had quite a collection of drawings, copies of the Brontë books signed by the authors and other keepsakes to which were added many items of clothing, including scarves, shawls, bows, mittens and collars. Arthur felt unable to include Charlotte's bed in the sale and arranged for it to be broken up and thrown away. Robert Ratcliffe, Tabitha's son, on hearing what was happening, asked if he could have the two long fluted bedposts and Arthur agreed. Robert also managed to salvage the bedhead and the hangings and took all these pieces home to his father, who was able to rebuild the bed around them. It was used by Tabitha.[5]

Cragg issued advertisements to the cost of £3.9s. and arranged for the lots to be viewed on September 30th. The Bill of Sale was headed 'Mr Cragg has the honor (*sic*) to announce that he has received instructions to sell by auction on Tuesday, 1st October, 1861 at the Parsonage, Haworth, the valuable household furniture of the late Rev. Patrick Brontë, B.A.'.[6] Those who bought goods at the sale, which lasted two days, were mostly local people. The catalogue gives a fascinating insight into the domestic arrangements at the Parsonage. Among the more practical items sold were the bread fleak (used for drying oatcakes) which was bought by Mrs Betty Lambert, who had helped nurse Charlotte in her last illness; a meat hastener, sold for 2/-, which surely disproves the stories that the Brontës did not eat meat; the shower bath purchased by Ellen for Charlotte, which cost £5, was knocked down for only 6/9. Very significantly, there were a number of bedpans, Doctor bottles (*sic*) and a spittoon. Mr Cragg himself bought a number of items, including a book of Brontë poems for 1/6. In all there were 485 lots. Arthur had the agony of knowing that they had all been examined and commented upon by neighbours, friends and complete strangers. The sale made £115 13s. 11d of which he received £103 9s. 11d after expenses and fees, plus half a crown (2/6d) from the teacher at the National School for all the waste paper. Shortage of materials in schools is nothing new!

Not everything had been sold or given away. Arthur would have needed the services of a carrier or shipper for the many possessions of sentimental value he was taking to his new life:

Charlotte's rosewood writing desk, her work box, her paint box; Charlotte's carefully preserved wedding dress and gloves, her portrait by Richmond and a photograph of the Parsonage. He packed Brontë manuscripts, juvenilia, water-colours and samplers by the Brontë sisters and Leyland's plaque of Branwell. Furniture included the birchwood rocking chair, an armchair, a small mahogany table, the grandfather clock and, finally, Patrick's gun.

The heart seems to have been taken out of Arthur. He did not apply for a new living but chose to remove himself far away, back to his childhood home with his Aunt Harriette, whom he regarded as his mother.

The two servants were now out of work. Eliza found herself a new position and Arthur offered Martha a job in Ireland. Having settled everything, and seen his goods off, there was no more to be done than to lock up and leave. Accompanied by Mr Brontë's dog, Plato, and his memories, he quietly left Haworth to begin a new life.

- 13 -

Return to Banagher and Second Marriage

Aunt Harriette was now a widow; her husband had died of asthma while Arthur was still at Trinity College. The family had retained Cuba Court and the school, and by this time the Bell's second son, the Rev. James Bell, had taken over the headmastership. He was living at Cuba Court, and his aunt with her daughter, Mary Anna, had moved into The Hill House, near the church at the top of the hill in Banagher.

The house is still there, though considerably altered and enlarged. At the time Arthur went there it was somewhat smaller in size than Haworth Parsonage, not at all like the stately Cuba Court, but it was pleasantly situated. A curved drive led to the front door and there was a gardener's cottage, stable and ice house. Indoors, the staircase ascended from a narrow hall at a right angle. There were four small bedrooms, one of which became known as Martha's room, whether she was there or not. The drawing room and the dining room were on the ground floor and the kitchen was in the basement. The outlook from the back was of fields and trees. At this small but pleasant house, Arthur, Plato and, later, Martha received a warm welcome.

When his belongings arrived from Haworth, Aunt Harriette and Mary Anna let him arrange them around the house to suit his own taste. The Haworth grandfather clock stood at the turn of the stairs, just as it had at the Parsonage. Nearby he placed Leyland's plaque of Branwell on the wall. In the dining room Patrick's old gun stood in a corner by the door and a photograph of Haworth Parsonage hung above the sideboard. The portrait of Charlotte and one of Thackeray held places of honour in the dining room, which was decorated with many of the pictures painted by the three sisters. In a glass-fronted bookcase Arthur kept his collection of Brontë books. He carefully put Charlotte's wedding dress, her tiny white gloves fastened with a pearl button at the wrist, her small square-toed black shoes and her going-away bonnet with the pink roses into a chest in the lobby. At almost every turn was some reminder of Charlotte.

Martha arrived after working a short while for Dr Ingham.[1] She found the kitchen quite different from that cosy room at Haworth; it was in the basement with only a small back window and it was dark, damp and gloomy. Despite the fact that it had a large fireplace, it could be very cold. The prevailing wind blew through cracks in the door, and, to counteract this, it was covered in layers of newspaper stuck one on top of the other.

Martha's role in the household was that of housekeeper-companion. She oversaw the other servants and sometimes baked sponge cakes to her own old Haworth recipe, for which she was renowned throughout the district. She found it easier to deal with the servants than did either Aunt Harriette or Mary Anna; the house ran more efficiently when she was there and they were quite happy to leave her to it.

Arthur settled into the life of a small country farmer – he never sought a clerical post again. He supervised the men on Aunt Harriette's 20 acres and joined in local activities. Arthur remained in touch with Haworth and on 5th November, 1861, he wrote to a clerical friend, 'There are repairs going on at the Parsonage, I understand – I dare say I shall scarce know it when I see it , but it will not be the same to me. I am busy farming in a very small way; we have two cows, a heifer and a calf. It affords me some little employment – the Rheumatism is still troublesome.' John Greenwood, despite previous differences, had written to him, appraising him of the 'goings on' in Haworth and he replied without rancour saying, 'As far as I am concerned I have benefited very much by the change – my health is much better than it has been for some time – Martha is also stronger than she was, so that on the whole I am quite satisfied with the turn matters took.' His life was much less fraught and he seemed to take to his new environment naturally.

In 1862 he returned to Haworth for a visit, staying with his old friends, the Grants. While there he visited Martha's mother and Tabitha. He kept in touch with the people back in Ireland, writing to Martha, advising her about her railway share dividends, and telling her that her mother was sending an apron and some stockings she had asked for. This was the beginning of a long correspondence between them which resumed whenever Martha was away, and which lasted until her death.[2] Arthur's letters were in a friendly, natural style, telling of the everyday happenings at Banagher and advising her on any problems. Her first visit home took place at the end of that year and his letters contained more advice on her (very few) shares, described Christmas at The Hill House, when the servants, Abbey and Julia, received new dresses which looked 'very nice indeed', reported the purchase of a new cow for £14 and enclosed a cheque for Martha and her mother to buy themselves Christmas presents.

Martha regularly made long visits to Ireland, dividing her time between there and Haworth. Banagher was a rural community, very unlike the more industrialised Haworth and nearby Keighley, and she was usually charged with commissions to fulfil for items that were cheaper or more readily available there. She was asked to bring back with her such diverse and homely items as a pewter plate for taking iron mould out of linen, eight yards of fine warm flannel for vests, black and white tweed, a pair of light clogs, a round cake tin and a cog wheel with 36 cogs for the washing machine. These were manufactured in Keighley and it was likely that a Keighley machine was another of the items Arthur had brought with him.

When Martha's mother was ill Arthur sent money to buy comforts for her, adding, 'if you need any more do not hesitate to ask me for it.' He continued to give her advice on her investments, on dealing with awkward lodgers, on the sale of her mother's house and many other practical matters, but, when she wrote to ask him for one of Charlotte's 'little books' for a friend, he could not bring himself to send one. He wrote back to her, 'I got one out to enclose to you but when I looked at the hand writing I could not bear to part with it.' Not even to Martha could he let any part of Charlotte go. When Martha's health began to fail he offered her a home at The Hill House: 'I wish you could come and reside as you are not strong enough for the work you have to do. There is no necessity to work when you can have a comfortable house with us and the means of visiting your friends whenever you wish.' When she died, in Haworth, at the age of 52, Arthur was deeply distressed.

Arthur returned from his visit to the Grants on 10th September in time for one of Banagher's major social events, the Great Fair.[3] It started on September 15th and continued for four days. This annual event saw an influx of people into the town, with side shows, stalls of all descriptions, fortune tellers and pedlars. The first day of the fair was given over to the sale of horses. The horse fair occupied the main street on both sides and stretched beyond the town, The sheep fair on the second day took place on Fair Green; the cattle in the same place on the third day and the fourth day was given over to the sale of pigs and a general country fair for the enjoyment of everyone. Even the children were given time off school to join in the fun; it was an event impossible to ignore. Altogether Banagher held nine fairs every year, the September one the most important, and, although he was only farming in a small way, Arthur used the opportunity to meet and talk to the other farmers and view the horses parading in front of The Hill House.

By this time, 1862, Arthur was 43 years of age. As the only man, he was regarded, in accordance with the thinking of the time, as the head of the household, even though the house belonged to Aunt Harriette, and he was deferred to in all things. He became a handyman around the house and fitted a water pump in the kitchen to the delight of Julia and Abbey, the servants, who found it 'a great convenience to have it so near to them'.

Mary Anna was 32. Arthur had always liked his cousin who had been a pretty, lively girl, with big brown eyes, but was now crippled by a riding accident and arthritis. She in her turn had always admired Arthur and, inevitably, as time passed they became drawn together. Aunt Harriette, who was now 61, could see the advantages of encouraging the friendship. If Arthur married Mary Anna, her daughter would have a secure future and they would have a dependable man about the house and farm. Eventually, in 1864 and nine years after Charlotte's death, he proposed to Mary Anna and was accepted. It seems to have been much more a marriage of convenience than of passion and the wedding was to be a quiet occasion, befitting the fact that for Arthur it was a second marriage. As with his wedding to Charlotte, he had obtained a special licence so that no banns had to be called.

He and Mary Anna were married at St Paul's Church over the road from The Hill House on 26th August, 1864, by Mary Anna's brother, Rev. Joseph Bell. The witnesses were Major Adamson, her uncle and Rev. V. Wetherall, the Rector of Banagher and a friend of Arthur.[4] The honeymoon was to be spent in Bangor, North Wales, the very place he had visited with Charlotte. It seems a very strange choice and Mary must have been very understanding to agree to this idea. He wrote to Martha, whilst on honeymoon in North Wales, without a hint of sentiment, 'We were married on August 25th and arrived the following day. We intend to remain a few days longer. We have not had good weather and have not seen much of the neighbourhood.' He went on to advise Martha, 'I don't think Jemmy Witham would be a good match for you. Be careful how you commit yourself', and then very chattily to describe recent happenings at Banagher, finishing by adding, 'We have built a room over the room off the parlour. It will make a good bedroom.'

- 14 -

Life in Banagher

On their return to The Hill House Arthur and Mary settled down
to married life. Mary had no illusions about Arthur's feelings for
Charlotte. In later life she would tell how Arthur had said he had
buried his heart with his first wife, and that he was devotedly
attached to her, guarding her fame as far as he could.[1] This she
accepted, at least on the surface, with equanimity. The only bone
of contention between them was the fact that Mary could not
bear to have animals in the house and did not like dogs, whereas
Arthur had always had one or more and could not understand
her attitude. She did, however, put up with some of his other
foibles. Sometimes she would see him surreptitiously feeling his
pulse – a doctor had once told him he had a weak heart and he
wanted to be certain it was functioning correctly! He also had a
penchant for crunching lump sugar, of which he was inordinately
fond. They had, however, been living in the same house for some
time and these habits and likes and dislikes must have been
known to each other before they were married.

Aunt Harriette's 20 acres did not really occupy Arthur's full
time and as a married man he wanted his own property. In March
1865, seven months after his marriage, he wrote to Martha, 'I
have some intention of taking a small farm, if I can get one with
a suitable house. I have been to look at one or two – I should like
something more to do than I have here.' Five months later he
still had not found anywhere suitable. There was discussion in
the family as to whether Mary and Arthur would remain at The
Hill House or not. He wrote to Martha, 'I don't know we shall
remain here but likely not.' The weather in 1865 had been bad
and the crops were in danger of serious damage. Aunt Harriette
would obviously miss the couple if they moved out and devised an
answer to the problem: she transferred the house and land into
Arthur's name. Now he was the master in his own right, and,
instead of talk of moving, he was looking to buy or rent more
land to increase the acreage. However, being a man of property
was not without its drawbacks. The next year he had to put off a

115

planned trip to England in order to have the roof repaired. The whole thing had to be taken off and replaced and a number of other repairs made to the fabric at not inconsiderable expense.

The Rev. James Bell, his cousin, had taken over the headship of the Royal Free School at Cuba House in 1849, although he was not ordained until 1852. The income from the Royal Free School was a stipend plus the rents from 204 acres, around £160. From this he had to pay the rent for Cuba House, which was leased at £113. 15s. p.a., provide for the maintenance of the buildings and furnishings and also the board of the boys. While it was nominally a free school, he was therefore very much dependent on private pupils who paid substantial fees. Demand for places at the school was declining and at the same time he was experiencing difficulty collecting the rents.[2]

James decided to seek a curacy and in 1865 was told he would be appointed to Ballymore, 20 miles away. Arthur, writing to Martha, described the new living as prettily situated, but said both church and parsonage were small. When Christmas came in 1865 James told the remaining pupils he was leaving and they were not to return. The proposed curacy did not mature for over a year, during which time he continued to draw his stipend and collect rents.

The Commissioners for the School protested that he had closed it; he countered this with sophistry, contending he had not – there just were no pupils. The situation continued until January, 1867, when he was forced to leave the school following an enquiry by the Commissioners.

Aunt Harriette had had a connection with Cuba House since her husband bought the headmastership in 1821, although other headmasters were employed between his death in 1839 and James taking over in 1849. The fuss and argument and the unseemly manner of his departure must have been keenly felt by her and all at The Hill House. In May, 1866, Mr Brontë's old dog, Plato, had died, severing one of the remaining links with Haworth. Then Martha's mother died and, in August, Arthur invited Martha to rejoin them, which she did in October following the sale of her mother's property. They were always pleased to see Martha, who acted as a very efficient housekeeper and her bustling presence would help take their minds off the family problems. This time Martha stayed with them for just over a year.

Mrs Arthur Bell, Aunt Harriette's daughter-in-law, and her

three children came to stay in July, 1868. They had arrived home from India in the spring and were looking for accommodation. In the meantime they were visiting their relatives. Arthur had intended to visit England that year, but, in view of their guests, his trip was cancelled. Originally they were expected to stay for two months, but the stay stretched to three. Arthur was normally pleasant to children but seemed to find the company wearing in the small house. Not only had it spoilt his plans for a visit to England, but he had also had to write to Martha at the beginning of September asking her to postpone her arrangements to join them in Banagher for another extended stay, as they, 'could not make her as comfortable as usual'. Later, on 24th September, 'Mrs Bell is still here, nor do I know the precise date of her departure. Most likely a week or ten days. I have written about steamers next month and will fix a date (for you) to come.' He wrote again on 6th October to advise her that Mrs Arthur Bell had left and suggesting the travel arrangements for a visit. In addition to the usual requests, he also asked her to order a 'wringing and mangling machine from Ben. Pay 32/- for it.'[3]

Dr Arthur Bell had been left behind in India, where he was Surgeon of the 36th Regiment. Sadly, a year later, on 2nd October, 1869, he died of cholera at Peshawar. He was 41. A memorial to him was erected by his Regiment and can be seen in Banagher Church. This was another blow for the family, particularly for Aunt Harriette, whose eldest son, Alan, had died at the Cape in September, 1868, after a three-day illness. Grieving was not over for Harriette and her family, for in 1870 her youngest son died aged 31. For the third year in a row Mary Anna had lost a brother and Arthur one of his cousins.

Arthur and Mary had a very wide circle of family and friends; they were very hospitable and welcomed visitors to their home. Colonel Adamson, Mary's uncle, often came over from Dublin to stay and Joseph Bell's wife and daughters sometimes stayed with them for the entire summer. Both Arthur and his wife were very fond of children, although they never had any of their own. His niece, Ethel, recalled that there was always a 'kind and affectionate welcome for the small visitor'.[4] One of Joseph's daughters remembered in old age how they all 'reverenced the memory of Charlotte Brontë who wrote the wonderful books in the glass fronted book case in the drawing room – Aunt Mary had given us permission to read the books, but I always had a fear of hurting my uncle if he should see me reading one of them, so I would hastily conceal it in his presence.'[5] Even the children were aware of Arthur's undiminished feelings towards Charlotte.

A young man who had reason to remember one of his visits to them was Arthur's nephew. He was seated speaking to his Aunt Mary in the drawing room, which was arranged with a table below Charlotte's portrait hung in the centre of the wall. Beyond that was his Aunt's sofa. Suddenly, for no apparent reason, the portrait fell from the wall, skipped the table and hit Mary, much to everyone's shock and surprise. Fortunately, neither she nor the picture suffered any damage, but she thought it was a very strange incident and he never forgot it.[6]

The only visitors whom Arthur came to dislike were some of the Americans who later in his life came to The Hill House in increasing numbers. They wanted to speak to Arthur but tended to ignore Mary altogether. She laughed at this and said she didn't mind, but their rudeness annoyed Arthur so much that he eventually refused to see any more such callers.[7]

Content with his country lifestyle and kept busy on the farm, Arthur rarely left Banagher. Mary often stayed with the Adamsons at their lodgings in Dublin and seemed to enjoy the opportunity to sample life in the big city, and the Adamsons returned the visits. On one such occasion, Arthur, as usual giving Martha all the news, wrote, 'It was the annual fair but not so many visitors as usual. The Col. and Miss Adamson were staying but they had to leave quickly as Mrs Henson [owner of their rooms in Dublin] was giving up the house. They have not found lodgings yet.' Mary's visits to Dublin were curtailed until they were re-settled. She missed the occasional glimpses of city life but it did not affect Arthur, who was happy at home. As time went by his dislike of travel grew, particularly with regard to the sea crossing to England. He was even making excuses to Martha for not visiting Haworth, 'I would like to come but I dread the crossing. I am generally so sick.' Although he was putting Haworth behind him, he could not forget Charlotte. He read every article written about her that he could find, even though these reminders left him quiet and withdrawn for several days afterwards.

As well as the guests who stayed at the house, the couple invited friends and neighbours to play whist, have tea or supper, or just to chat. Arthur became very friendly with Rev. J. J. Sharrard and his family. He had been appointed Rector in 1885 and the two men found they shared many common interests.

Arthur was included in such events as the children's Christmas party at the vicarage where he was given a little fancy bag full of his favourite sugar lumps, at which 'he was very tickled'. Mr Sharrard persuaded him to take a service in the Church, but it had been so long since Arthur had stood before a congregation that he was painfully nervous, and no further attempts were made to persuade him into the pulpit. Even so, he remained religious all his life. Every night he would kneel to pray at the chair which Charlotte had used for the same purpose during her life – another of his precious reminders of his first marriage which he had brought with him from Haworth.[8] He was a regular attender at St Paul's and was a member of the Select Vestry of the Banagher Parish Church. One of the few occasions when he lost his temper was when he caught a group of youths playing pitch and toss outside the church on a Sunday afternoon. He upbraided them with such anger they sheepishly fled.

Helen, the Sharrards' daughter, was very fond of Arthur,[9] nicknaming him 'Baboo Nick' and described him as a dear old man, very quiet and very shy. She recalled how he would bring her a bunch of the first lilies-of-the-valley to bloom and how, when they went on holiday, he would come out to wave them off. He had a bad tempered little dog, a mongrel terrier, called Pincher, who went everywhere with him but was never allowed into the house. Pincher was one of a succession of dogs owned by Arthur, one of his favourite's being Stray, the sheep dog, who accompanied him on his walks around his fields. He still retained his love of nature and would never cut down a tree.[10] The house became surrounded by large trees, far different from the open aspect it shows today.

By the 1870s, Haworth Church was in a bad way, suffering from damp and dry rot and was gloomy and inconvenient after various piece-meal alterations, largely due to lack of funds when the church had been part of Bradford Parish. The incumbent, Rev. John Wade, had now been upgraded to Rector, and, after, considering various plans for very extensive and expensive repairs, the decision was taken to demolish the church and build a new one on the same site. As with all such proposals, this stirred up controversy, some saying that the Rector was destroying an architectural masterpiece; others saying it was about time the rotten, decaying, unhealthy church was replaced before it became dangerous. Rumours abounded that graves would be disturbed or removed, including that of the Brontë family.[11] It was proposed that, after carefully noting the site of the graves, the wooden floor would be replaced by a thick layer of concrete. Mr Wade wrote to Arthur, soliciting his support. Arthur replied:

'Dear Sir,
I had seen the articles in the *"Standard"* & *"Daily Telegraph"* before the receipt of your letter. Let me assure you that I did not for a moment believe that you ever entertained, much less gave utterance to the unkind sentiments towards the Brontë family attributed to you by the writers of those articles. That you should object to have your privacy destroyed by the constant influx of strangers into your house is not to be wondered at. I suffered from the inconvenience myself, but tho I felt constrained to submit to it, that is no reason why you should be expected to do so likewise.

The enlargement of the house seemed to me to have been carried out with great judgement for, whilst affording you the additional accommodation required for your large household, it left the distinctive features of the old building unaltered. When I first heard of the proposed New Church I hoped that it would be erected on a new site and that the old one endeared to me by many associations would be allowed to stand. As however the circumstances you mention seem to make this impossible, I certainly cannot say that I "wish the inhabitants of Haworth to be forever condemned to worship in a building which is both unsafe and inconvenient". I thank you very much for the assurance that special care shall be taken to prevent any disturbance of the remains of those so dear to me. If the proposed tomb over the graves is carried out I shall be glad to contribute towards defraying the expense.

Many thanks for letting me see the plans which seem very suitable. I return them by this post.

Believe me
Very truly yours
A. B. Nicholls.'[12]

The proposal for a tomb over the graves was not carried out and, when in 1881 Sidney Biddell pressed for a memorial on the site of the graves, sentiment had moved against him. Wade, himself, was not in favour of a new memorial as he did not wish to encourage more tourists and Arthur by now was only lukewarm about the idea. His preferred view was that, if there was to be a new memorial, it should be to his wife only, and not to the whole family.

Sidney Biddell, an avid admirer of the Brontës, was a landowner at Fairholme near Stroud who had trained for the bar but never practised. His claim to fame was that he had rowed for Cambridge in the first Oxford and Cambridge Boat Race. He wrote to Ellen Nussey, 'I am in correspondence with Mr Wade, the Rector of Haworth, about erecting a memorial to the Brontë family in his new Church. Mr Nicholls contemplates erecting a memorial to his wife only but would probably not object to its being a memorial to the three sisters, so that the outside public could take part in it.'[13] This was just what Wade and Arthur did not want as any one who really knew the two men would realise. Having been in correspondence with Mr Wade, Biddell wrote once more to Ellen in 1882, 'I have not had the heart to reply to Mr Wade's letters. There is such a wheel within wheel in everything in connection with Haworth, its Rector and its new church, that I have not had the courage to attempt more than a simple memorial cross or plate.' He went on to say that he had called on George Smith, the publisher, but was told that 'he would have nothing to do with any memorial and was far too busy to be troubled by any such matter . . . If people who knew her . . . will do nothing, what can I do? If anything could show up Mr Nicholls as being a monster, I am sure it would be his lukewarmness in this matter. He cares to do nothing and, in one respect I am glad of it, for if he did, I certainly wouldn't want any thing to do with it.'[14] Biddell, who seems to have absorbed some of Ellen's spleen, obviously did not understand Arthur's feelings.

His dream of a fine memorial came to nothing and, in the end, he had to settle for the small brass plate which can be seen in the church on the site of the Brontë vault recording the names of Charlotte and Emily.

Attempts at Further Biographies

Ellen Nussey was not entirely happy with *The Life of Charlotte Brontë*, although perversely she blamed Mr Nicholls rather than Mrs Gaskell. She felt she had not had the credit or the remuneration she deserved. For some time she had had the idea of publishing her own version and had even gone so far as consulting M.Heger on this but had not received any encouragement.[1] In January, 1869, she decided to take matters further and wrote to George Smith, offering to provide some letters, and sought his opinion on publication. He replied,

'My Dear Madam,
I am afraid I must suggest a difficulty in regard to the publication of Miss Brontë's letters to you which may not have occurred to your mind. The right to print those letters (otherwise the copyright in these letters) belongs to Mr Nicholls and not to you. The letters themselves are your property and Mr Nicholls cannot claim them from you, but you cannot print them without his permission. This permission, I fear, will not be easy to obtain but, if the letters are suitable for publication, it might be, at all events, worthwhile to endeavour to get Mr Nicholls' consent to their publication and I shall be very glad to see the letters you have copied if you will do me the favour of sending them.
Believe me.
My dear Madam,
Yours very faithfully,
G. Smith.'[2]

Ellen sent copies of a substantial number of letters to Smith. He wrote to her on 21st January and at this time was still referring to 'we' with regard to obtaining Arthur's permission to publish. Charlotte's portrait was then being exhibited at South Kensington on loan from Arthur and he advised Ellen, 'I shall endeavour to get his address from them [the museum authorities] as we may wish to communicate about the letters.'[3] The fact that Arthur had lent the Richmond portrait to the South Kensington (now the Victoria and Albert) Museum showed that he was not averse to publicity regarding Charlotte provided it was done in a reasonable manner.

In the meantime Ellen was asking George Smith to recover from Arthur any of her letters to Charlotte which she felt sure he was keeping. As she had kept the letters she had received from Charlotte she was quite sure that she would have kept hers and now Arthur was hoarding them! She wrote to George Smith that she had letters which he [Arthur] would 'in his place give almost a fortune to possess – besides one from Mr Brontë written under the sobriquet of the old favourite dog. If you think it right you can give him a hint that he has not all the power on his side and there is an obligation in kindness which is never ignored by true hearted people.'[4]

George Smith, probably alarmed at what she might write and the letters that she might include, suggested to Ellen the publication in the *Cornhill Magazine* of 'a brief and simple narrative' of her friendship illustrated by some of the letters. He went on, 'I think Mr Nicholls could not make any objection to such a publication, especially if it took place in the *Cornhill Magazine*. Indeed I could venture to print your article in the Magazine without communicating with him.'[5]

After another exchange of letters, back-pedalling further, he wrote,

'I may say that the doubt I felt as to Mr Nicholls approving the publication of some portions of these letters is confirmed by the tone of your allusions to him. I have not had any communication with Mr N. for some time and should not have thought of writing to him on the subject of your letters as any application to him more properly should come from you, especially as you desire to get back any letters of yours. But I think that we might venture to print such articles as I suggested without applying to Mr Nicholls on the subject.'[6]

He goes on to say that for two or three articles she might expect to receive '£50 or thereabouts', much less than the £125 for one article she had been expecting.

Ellen wrote to him on 27 February, 1869, 'The allusions to my own letters led me to think you had some knowledge of their existence through Mr N. Charlotte said before her marriage that she would destroy all former correspondence but I was led very seriously to doubt her having carried out this instruction from some little episodes in Mr N's subsequent behaviour. He discovered something about your Mr Taylor which sent him over hither in an excited state a month after his wife's death. He did not find me at home happily – but he wrote Miss Wooler on the subject – fortunately she knew little – his next move was to get me into his neighbourhood to stay with some intimate friends . . . It was a great shock to me realising that he had been ransacking his wife's things speedily after losing her – unfavourable impression deepened still more afterwards by what seemed a most selfish appropriation of everything to himself . . . his notes to me became less and less civil in the time to Mr Brontë's death when I ceased to write at all. I feel an insuperable aversion to write to him even for the attaining (if I could) of my own letters.'[7]

The above letter owes more to Ellen's paranoia as far as Arthur is concerned than a realistic account of his actions. Most of the information about Charlotte and Mr Taylor was to come in due course from Ellen's letters and, if Arthur was making enquiries, it was probably from something Mr Brontë let slip.

Learning that she would have to approach Mr Nicholls herself and, in view of the small remuneration, she wrote to George Smith and asked him to return the letters. No article was published. However, a year later, through the intermediary of John Bigelow, a diplomat and literary editor, the letters were published in *Hours at Home*, the magazine of the American publishers, Scribners, and her reminiscences in its successor, *Scribners Monthly* for May, 1871. Because there was then no copyright agreement with America, Ellen was thus able to avoid, what was to her, the distasteful task of having to obtain Arthur's permission.

Her next brush with Arthur was over her venture with Thomas Wemyss Reid, at that time editor of the *Leeds Mercury*. She had heard him lecturing on Charlotte and found he was intending to write a memoir on the subject. She wrote, 'It is a very sad injustice to her memory that one so pure and excellent as she was, should have anything connected with her printed Life that is unsuited for the reading of the young innocent. One volume such as you could produce would make her Life vastly more taking as well as doing more justice to her memory. If you will enlarge your intended biography to a vol. I will put as much as I possibly can into your hands – You shall have almost all her letters to refer to & any other help I can give you – Mrs Gaskell's *Life of C.B.* is losing its hold upon the public generally, but a single volume from a fresh writer would awaken (I think) a new and universal interest – do think of this – and after thinking consent.'

She continued to lay on flattery with a trowel:

'I am certain of this, your Monograph is a thousand times more valuable than Mrs G's memoirs and that it will be through you that Charlotte's noble life will be estimated in years to come. Charlotte and I used to remark that all the people who attracted us were people of very full moral development in their heads – rounded and full, as laughingly we said "we ourselves are". I noticed this in your prose the first, but you have the other grand quality of intellect – You have this grand magnet to a gifted being like Charlotte – this explains to me your wonderful power of accurate perception, & talented description of a person you have never seen. Don't think I flatter (I can't do it). It is to me as marvellous as it is gratifying for my dear friend's sake.'

She went on to end with a complaint about Mr Nicholls,

'I should think Mr Nicholls will bite his nails at the last article, but he had better stop there. "Currer Bell" was none of his, she belongs far more to the public than to him in that character. Tell him to read the life of the Prince Consort. What indeed have the pure and the upright to shrink from – they will have to face the great Searcher of hearts before all the world in the great day of account, then why fear the little world of the present time.'[8]

Wemyss Reid had arranged for a version of the monograph to be published in *Macmillan's Magazine* over the months of August to October. Arthur saw or was shown these articles and was understandably upset. He wrote a short sharp note to Wemyss Reid who passed the news to Ellen: 'I have received a peremptory letter from Mr Nicholls desiring me to inform you of his displeasure. Poor man! I have written him a civil answer

which I hope may turn away his wrath.'⁹ A few days later when
he wrote again, Arthur was mollified:
   'I have had another letter from Mr Nicholls, much
   more moderate in tone than the first, thanking me
   very sincerely for all I have written about his wife.'
This is a reasoned and courteous letter and in view of
the 'dog in the manger' attitude often attributed to
Arthur we feel it is worth printing this in full:

'Private   Hill House
                                      Banagher
                                      Ireland
                                      6 Nov 1876
Sir
I deferred writing to you again until I had seen the
concluding part of your Monograph.
   'I do not object to anything you have written about
my wife; on the contrary I thank you very sincerely for
the high tribute you have paid to her character &
genius; but I do object to the publication of the letters
in the Oct No referring to Mr X—. It is true I wrote to
Miss Nussey requesting her to permit Mrs Gaskell to
see the correspondence & to make extracts from it –
but had I known that these letters were in existence I
should have asked her to destroy them, as I had done
Miss Wooler; who however had anticipated my wishes
in this respect –
   'I was aware that some letters had been published in
the United States, but I failed to obtain a copy of the
periodical in which they appeared – I regret to hear
that these were [the] documents, but I feel that I am
myself to blame for not having cautioned Miss Nussey
that my wife's letters were not hers for publication – I
could not however imagine that she would have been
so unmindful of what was due to the memory of the
dead and the feelings of the living –
   'There is one passage in page 16 of Nov No,
beginning "once she failed", which from its obscurity
is I think liable to misconstruction. I should be obliged
by you revising it –
   'I do not know from what source you derived your
information respecting Mr Brontë – in my opinion the

character is very much overdrawn – I knew him intimately for more than sixteen years – seven of these spent under the same roof with him , and yet I never witnessed any ebullitions of passion such as you describe as habitual with him and venting themselves in the discharge of pistols against the doors of the outhouses of the Parsonage – nor have I ever heard him talk on "the subject of his conquests over the hearts of the ladies of his congregation" – that he like all of us had his peculiarities there is no doubt; but it grieves me that he should be represented to the world as "a strange compound of good & evil" – and as one "not without some good acknowledged by all who knew him" – that his opposition to my marriage caused me much suffering is quite true, but to myself personally he never uttered an unkind or angry word – I revere his memory as that of one of the truest and best friends I ever had –

    I remain Sir
        faithfully yours
           A. B. Nicholls'.[10]

About the same time Ellen was also writing to Wemyss Reid, her letter mostly a tirade about Arthur:

'A *low feverish*	Laneside Gommersall
kind of cold has	
possessed for some	Nov 3rd 1876
days and made me	
very <u>stupid</u>	

My dear Sir
The intelligence of your having received a peremptory letter from Mr Nicholls did not surprise me in the least for I know he is pugnaciously inclined. Charlotte used to say, "he enjoyed 'whacking' the boys in the schools", he is also very <u>pertinacious</u> – I am afraid if you do not show him you have a st<u>ro</u>ng fi<u>st</u> yourself he will still wax bold. If I were you I would ask Lord Houghton to take him in hand.

    'If he has any honour in him he must hold himself bound to respect his dicta in <u>this</u> ma<u>tt</u>er for if I remember rightly he was offered some preferment from Lord H. after his marriage with Charlotte. I am deeply obliged to him for wishing <u>his</u> dis<u>plea</u>sure to be made known to me – I wish he could see how concerned I am! I did not suspect him of such vanity. He was far too pig-headed and obtuse to be mated with a being like Charlotte – but for his sel<u>fish</u>ness & w<u>ant</u> of per<u>cep</u>tion I believe Charlotte would have been alive now, disinterested affection would have given him perception but he had it not. Against anything he can have to say there are his own words of respect for himself and Mr Brontë for material for Mrs Gaskell's memoir also Mrs Gaskell's letter after her visit to Haworth – if he do not beware he will have her retribution! There is no knowing what that villainous old Mr Brontë put into his head, I have never liked to tell you, but perhaps its best since you know so much, that you should know the worst – the old villain! for I can never think of this episode without the most contemptuous feeling, & I believe in one particular Mary Taylor had similar experience for she spoke of him as that "wicked old man". The consummate vanity of the man made him equal to any artifice. In revenge he did his best to alienate Charlotte's faithful heart from her faithful friend even when I was in the house, the last visit before her marriage (except the one made <u>with</u> Miss Wooler for the marriage – She turned upon him with rage as we breakfasted when he made some kind of hypocritical remark to me on the vicissitudes of life; of course this cannot be alluded to, only it may explain any disagreeable comments from Mr N <u>as from whence they arise</u>.'[11] The underlinings are Ellen's.

At this point she suddenly switched off the anger and the rest of the letter deals quite calmly with other matters.

Wemyss Reid was always polite and courteous in his letters to Ellen and was honest and straightforward in his dealings, which was more than could be said for later writers. He received £100 for the two articles and the book and, after consultation with others, paid her and Miss Wooler £33. 6s. 8d. for the loan of the letters.[12] She remained on friendly terms with him and in 1884 asked him about placing the letters in the British Museum. He told her that he had spoken about them to one of the Museum

Trustees, Lord Houghton, who did not encourage it, 'They would be open to everybody and perhaps an unscrupulous use might be made of them . . . more could be made out of them when Mr Nicholls died, but not before, and even then it would need to be done very tenderly and discreetly.'

Her next move was lending letters to Rev. A. E. Wilkes who was to write a book on the Brontës, but she did not like his style and the attempt fell through. She got her letters back but believed he had kept some. He wrote, indignantly, 'Allow me to say that I scrupulously and religiously returned to you every letter written by the Brontës which you were kind enough to lend me – I did not retain one:- nor do I possess one line of their writing which ever belonged to you.'[13]

Ellen went on trying to publish new biographies and versions of the letters which would reflect her point of view. In 1885 she approached Horsfall Turner. She had told him she would leave the letters to him to be sold to provide a memorial in Birstall Church. He went ahead editing, typesetting and printing the letters over the next four years, but then she felt he was not dealing with them as she wished. She demanded their return and said she was not going to bequeath the letters to him. By now Turner had done much printing and, after a bitter dispute, the matter was settled by her solicitor; Ellen paid £100 to Turner and she took away the printed pages. Rev. John Ridley, a local clergyman, had rashly agreed to help her destroy the printed pages but was to regret this when he found out there were as many as 30,000 sheets, some flat, some part folded and some folded. He spent weeks of his spare time burning, pulping and burying and was 'glad for his own sake' when the task was done.[14] She kept a few copies that formed the basis of later attempts. Later it was said that the edition had been withdrawn because of a veto by Arthur, which again added to his reputation for making difficulties for biographers. This was not, in fact, the case: he had not even been in touch with Ellen or Horsfall Turner about publication.

Almost straight away, she got in touch with Augustine Birrell with a view to publishing in America. Whilst this would get round the possibility of Mr Nicholls vetoing the publication, she was advised that copies of the book could not legally be imported into this country if he objected. At the same time she was having discussions with Dr William Wright of Norwood in London on the copyright question and he had offered to buy the letters for

£50. In 1892 she broke off negotiations with Scribners. Wright's letters play on Ellen's hatred for Arthur but also show a deviousness inappropriate for a man of the cloth:

'Nicholls can stop publication of the letters. That being so it will be necessary to get his sanction.

'The barrister asked me, "Is he a beast?" I was obliged to answer that I thought he was. In fact he grabbed up everything at Haworth whether it belonged to him or not.'

He offered to negotiate for Ellen, saying,

'I might promise that if we published in England everything might be eliminated that might give him pain and I might let him have a few pounds, £5 or £10, for his consent and we should take care that his consent should be irrevocable – a gift can always be withdrawn unless some equivalent has been received.'[15]

Three days later he added:

'N must have been awfully commonplace. If the portrait in *Haworth Past and Present* is like him, you must have been shocked to see him husband of your brilliant friend. Surely it was beneficent providence that relieved her of his presences while she was still unaware of his wooden character.'[16]

Ellen moved from having a high regard for her latest adviser to deciding he was too presumptuous and once again broke off the relationship.

On to the scene came Mr C. K. Shorter, who was to take up the task of publication. In addition he introduced Ellen to Thomas J. Wise as someone who was interested in purchasing the letters and he offered her £100. At that time she wrote, 'A proper and true portrait of C.B. is very desirable in these days of evil inventions from people who certainly ought to know better . . . I intend to keep the original letters . . . for some time longer.'[17] However, only a few days later she fell to Mr Wise's importuning and accepted £125 for her letters reputed to number 400. She also lent other items to Clement Shorter to help him with his essay work but claimed these were not returned, and once more the situation descended into acrimony. Shorter returned a letter in his possession but the letters from Charlotte's death-bed had gone to Wise who insisted he had purchased them properly.

In 1895 Shorter did what no one else had thought to do. He wrote to Arthur and received, 'a cordial invitation to visit him in his Irish home'.[18] On 31st March, 1895, the fortieth anniversary of Charlotte's death, the two men met. Shorter, who could be charming and personable, received the 'cordial hand clasp of the man into whose keeping Charlotte Brontë had given her life. It was to be one of many visits and the beginning of an interesting correspondence.'[19] Arthur handed over all the papers he could find to the delighted Shorter who wrote, 'I found him [Arthur] in a home of supreme simplicity and charm, esteemed by all who knew him and idolised in his own household. It was not difficult to see why Charlotte Brontë had loved him and had fought down parental opposition on his behalf. The qualities of gentleness, sincerity, unaffected piety, and delicacy of mind are his; and he is beautifully jealous, not only for the fair fame of Currer Bell, but – what she equally would have loved – for her father, who also has had much undue detraction in the years that are past. That Mr Nicholls may long continue to enjoy the kindly charm of his Irish home will be the wish of all who have read of his own continuous devotion to a wife who must ever rank among the greatest of her sex.'

Clement Shorter's charm offensive turned to a genuine liking and the two men got on well together. In the following November Arthur sold the copyright in Charlotte's manuscripts to Shorter for the sum of £150. The deal was for the copyright in all the manuscripts which were then or might in future be in his hands over which Arthur had any rights, or which Shorter might receive from Ellen Nussey.[20] He had succeeded by friendliness where Ellen had failed, recognising, as Charlotte had written to Margaret Wooler many years before, that Arthur was, 'a man never indeed to be driven – but who may be led'.[21]

Thomas Wise, an associate of Shorter, bought through him a large collection of manuscripts from Arthur. He claimed to have paid £1,000 for them, but according to Shorter it was about £400. He proceeded to sell them and also Ellen Nussey's collection of Charlotte's letters, splitting up work which should have been kept together and passing off Branwell's work as Charlotte's in order to give it greater value, a mercenary act of vandalism.

Later Life and Death

A surprising facet of Arthur's character is found in his support for Gaelic football. The Harp and Banagher Football Club was founded in 1884. The initial list of subscribers contains 64 names. Arthur contributed the fifth highest amount with a subscription of 4/-, most of the others being only 1/- or 6d.[1]

The potato famine had resulted in a huge increase in Irish nationalism. One of the ways this had been manifested was in a renewed interest in native Irish games, particularly Gaelic football and hurling, leading to the formation of the Gaelic Athletic Association. It was predominantly a Catholic and Republican organisation; Protestants and Unionists tended to support such games as cricket and tennis and, in the eyes of many Protestants, the association was seen as subversive and a cover for Republicanism. Policemen were forbidden or dissuaded from joining, and those who did subscribe to local clubs signed themselves as 'A. Friend' to keep their names secret. One of the Catholic complaints was the tithe which they had to pay, along with everyone else, to support the Protestant Church of Ireland. Even so, Arthur gave generously to found the local club.

More normally, for a Protestant clergyman, we hear of his presence in 1893 at a special meeting of the Select Vestry of Banagher Parish Church which unanimously approved the protest of the General Synod against Gladstone's second Home Rule Bill. The Rector, Rev. J. J. Sharrard, was in the Chair and present were: Rev. A. B. Nicholls, B.A., Major T. P. St.George Armstrong, J.P., F. Plunket Dunne, J.P., Captain A. H. Burdett, J.P., Thomas Campion and Thomas Peart.[2]

A few days later a full meeting of Unionists took place at Cuba House where 'a large and thoroughly representative' attendance passed the following resolutions:

'That we the Loyalists of Banagher and surrounding districts in public meeting assembled, declare our unaltered loyalty to the person and throne of their

Gracious Majesty Queen Victoria, and desire that the legislative union of the United Kingdom be maintained.' and,

'That we protest against the principles of the Home Rule Bill now before Parliament, in the belief that the proposals of the Prime Minister, if passed into law, will prove disastrous alike to England and Ireland, resulting, as regards the latter country, in the establishment of mob law and the bankruptcy of the Irish Exchequer; and that we pledge ourselves to resist the passing of such measures into law by every means in our power, appealing to the British Government to assist us in this crisis.'

Although passed in the Commons, the Home Rule Bill was defeated in the House of Lords.

Since his return to Ireland Arthur had, apart from his brush with Wemyss Reid, remained aloof from literary circles. This was partly of his own choosing but also partly due to the fearsome reputation Ellen Nussey and Mrs Gaskell had given him. He had absorbed himself in his farming and local matters, but by 1895 he had given up farming and the family was living on the income from their investments. He did 'manage' a property for one of Mary Anna's relatives but this probably consisted of nothing more than collecting the rents, putting in hand minor repairs and rendering accounts. The most he would have received from this would have been a small honorarium, if anything at all. Interest rates were low and capital was being eaten away. The family was living in genteel poverty.

At the same time he was beginning to wonder what would happen to all his relics of Charlotte when he died. He wanted the Richmond portrait to go to the National Portrait Gallery, the various manuscripts books and documents to the South Kensington Museum (now the Victoria and Albert) and he was wanting to do what he could to ensure this while he was still able. Therefore, the visit from Shorter in 1895 came at a most opportune time for both of them and the two men got on well together. Shorter had been a civil servant but had switched to journalism and at this time was the editor of *The Illustrated London News*. He also founded *The Sketch,* and, later, *The Sphere,* and *The Tatler,* so in Arthur's opinion would have had a good reputation. They began a correspondence which was to last ten years, although it faded towards the end as Arthur became forgetful and too ill to write.

Arthur sold many items to Shorter, and through him to Thomas J.Wise, who at this time was still respected and was to be a future President of the Brontë Society. He was not to be disgraced for forgery and for his unscrupulous handling of Brontë relics until 1934. Arthur, writing to Shorter in June, 1895, to thank him for Wise's cheque, said he understood the destination of the letters was the South Kensington Museum. Wise has annotated this letter in pencil to the effect that he gave no such undertaking.[3] Although later in a letter of 28th December Arthur said he was satisfied with Mr Wise's assurances that the letters and manuscripts would be given to the nation he did not entirely trust him. In January, 1896, he lent Shorter six letters to Emily, one to Patrick and one to Miss Branwell with the admonition, 'Don't let Mr Wise appropriate them.'[4]

Shorter was usually seeking out more manuscripts or information and Arthur was happy to co-operate to help Shorter produce his book on the Brontës. Letters and writings seem to have been tucked away in little parcels in drawers, cupboards and wardrobes all over the house. He was, however, adamant that he had not had any of Ellen Nussey's letters to Charlotte, 'You may tell Miss Nussey that her letters never came into my possession and I assumed my wife burned them as soon as read.'[5] He was conscious of the problems letters could cause. With regard to one of Mary Taylor's letters to Charlotte he wrote, 'The contents are of a very private nature and therefore I did not send it with the others.' – 'I cannot bear the idea of making publick anything that could possibly hurt a person's feelings – I suffered too much from Mrs Gaskell's indiscretion.'[6] For his part Shorter supplied Arthur and Mary Anna with books and magazines and kept him in touch by sending cuttings of any articles on the Brontës.

As a result of this, on more than one occasion Arthur asked Shorter to disabuse authors of wrong impressions in their books or articles: to Birrell with regard to his relationship with Patrick, much on the same lines as Arthur had written to Wemyss Reid many years earlier, and also to Wemyss Reid himself, who had written an article, quoting Ellen Nussey, saying that he had objected to Charlotte writing another book . The book was *Emma*, another book about a school. 'I merely remarked critics could accuse her of repetition and she said "I shall change all that." You may therefore give an unqualified contradiction to the statement that I objected to my wife's work.[7]

Shorter visited him on four or five occasions over the years. In November Arthur sent his congratulations to Shorter on the announcement of his engagement to Dora Sigerson and on their wedding in June, 1896, sent a small present. In October Shorter's book, *Charlotte Brontë and Her Circle*, was published and a copy sent to Arthur who wrote, 'Thank you most sincerely for the kind and loving spirit in which you have treated a difficult and delicate subject.'[8]

Reginald Smith, the publisher and nephew of George Smith, also visited him on several occasions, once in 1898 to advise him that he was bringing out a new edition of the sisters' novels. Reginald Smith also asked Arthur, through Shorter, for permission to have a copy taken of the Richmond portrait to hang in the library of a ladies' college at Cambridge University. Arthur readily agreed and this was arranged. The same year Arthur wrote to Shorter with a rather pathetic request. He had discovered that a lock of Charlotte's hair was to be sold at Sotheby's. Would Shorter act for him in the matter of its return. He wanted it desperately. Shorter managed to obtain it and sent it to Arthur, who in conveying his thanks noted resignedly that, 'It is sadly reduced in size.'

In June, 1895, the Brontë Society was born, in order to preserve relics and manuscripts, and to establish a Brontë Museum. It had Arthur's sympathy but he did not wish to take an active part in its running. He had never been much of a one for travelling far from home and he particularly disliked the sea crossing. When W. T. Field, the Honorary Corresponding Secretary, invited him to the opening of the Museum in 1895 Arthur replied that he could not attend the ceremony as it would be too fatiguing at his advanced age.[9] He was then 77. He showed an interest in the work and meetings of the Brontë Society and corresponded regularly with Mr Field, who kept him informed of their doings and sent copies of their publications.

His once jet black hair was now snowy white and his full white beard gave him a venerable appearance. The people of Banagher were used to seeing his distinguished figure, wrapped in a large black cloak, visiting the post office, or leaning on his stick, his dog by his side, chatting to acquaintances in the street.

Respected and well known, he led a peaceful life which was a far cry from the turmoil of his years at Haworth. His Aunt Harriette was still living. She was now aged 94 and was set to reach the ripe old age of 100 before she died.

The potato famine had struck hard in Banagher in the 1840s when the population was reduced by starvation and emigration from 2,872 in 1841 to only 1,192 in 1871. During most of the remainder of the century Banagher was a depressed area. The Duke, later George V, and the Duchess of York paid a visit in 1897, seen by the Loyalists as a reward for their messages of support. The weather was atrocious. The party had travelled by boat down the Shannon in pouring rain and did little at Banagher but transfer to the royal train, much to the glee of the Home Rulers. One of the few people to meet the Royal party was Arthur's friend, little Helen Sharrard, who was five at the time and who presented the Duchess with a bouquet and the Duke with a buttonhole.

The Home Rule movement was very strong in King's County and, when the first county council elections were held in 1898 with all male householders and women being allowed to vote, the Home Rulers almost swept the board. They replaced the County Grand Jury, whose members had been selected by the High Sheriff of the county and were landowners and largely Unionist. The same year the distillery failed, and, when the next year, W. T. Field, Corresponding Secretary of the Brontë Society, wrote to Clement Shorter an account of his visit to Arthur, he said, 'What a fearful place Banagher is. The whisky distilleries have failed again (about a year ago) and the male population are absolutely destitute of occupation.'[10] He had had dinner with the Nicholls and on a more personal note wrote, 'He is wonderfully hale and well and is in his 81st year. It seems a pity we cannot persuade him to have a photo taken since it is 40 years since the last . . . I don't know that I got anything fresh out of the old gentleman, as I did not go in an interviewing spirit but simply to have a shake of his hand.'

The Boer War caused further problems in Ireland, some people campaigning against Irishmen joining the British army, although many did, and others even went out to fight for the Boers. Arthur was saddened by the carnage and he commented to Shorter, 'It's sad so many brave men have lost their lives for their Country. We have one nephew with Buller's force and another going out with the Imperial Yeomanry.'[11]

In January, 1902, he wrote to Mr Field commenting that the Society had had a good meeting at Morley and that he was much interested in the accounts of places referred to in *Jane Eyre*. He went on to say that his mother-in-law was 'tolerably well', having reached 100 on 6th October, and added that the quiet life they were now leading accounted for their longevity, the three inhabitants of the house 'tot up to 256 years.' He closed with his remembrances to Mrs Field. [12]

Aunt Harriette was not to be with them much longer. She died some five months later in June. In the year following her death, Arthur made his will.[13] It was a simple document which specified, 'The portrait of my late dear wife, by G. Richmond, I leave to the National Gallery. To my beloved wife the residue of my personal estate of every description. I make her my sole executrix. If my wife Mary dies before me I wish all my personal estate at the time of my death which I shall be possessed of, or entitled to, to go to my niece Violet Mary Bolster'. It was witnessed by his doctor, Robert Kerans, and his friend James Sharrard, Rector of Banagher, and dated 29 April 1903. Arthur's friendship with Mr Sharrard and his family continued for the rest of his life, and their daughter, Helen, often went for walks with him and his dogs. The old man and the small girl were great companions and she remembered him and his wife, Mary Anna, with great affection.

As time went on Arthur was failing both physically and mentally, and, when Mr Field invited him to the Brontë Society's 50th Commemoration of Charlotte's death in 1905, Mary Anna wrote in reply, 'Mr Nicholls has been very infirm and weakly for some time, and we are obliged to keep him very quiet, free from the least excitement, as his heart is very weak but, thank God, he suffers little pain and goes out a little every day. Still, we let him see few people, nor allow even our own relations to talk very much to him. We read for him but only of things of common interest. We never give him anything likely to excite or set him talking.'[14]

Although he became confused and childish, Mary Anna was always patient with him and cared for him devotedly, even when he was thinking of Charlotte and of meeting her again after his death, muttering over and over, 'I wonder how it will be?'

At the end of November, 1906, Arthur fell ill. The doctor diagnosed bronchitis, which, considering his age and frailty, was very serious. He was confined to bed. Mary Anna, lame and suffering from arthritis, could not care for him herself and a nurse, Kathleen McLean, was hired. Her assistance was not required for long. As he slipped in and out of consciousness Arthur's last thoughts were of his beloved first wife. Soon he would know the answer to his oft repeated question – he would know how it would be. After four days of illness it was Nurse McLean who heard his whispered dying words, 'Charlotte – Charlotte,' the name of his never forgotten first love.

Aftermath

Arthur Bell Nicholls is buried to the north-east side of St Paul's Church, Banagher, close to the graves of other members of the Bell family. He shares his grave with Mary Anna who died in 1915 aged 85. The grave is marked by a white stone cross with the Inscription:

UNTIL THE DAY BREAK
AND THE SHADOWS FLEE AWAY
Canticles Ch2 V17
IN
LOVING MEMORY
OF
THE REV^d ARTHUR BELL NICHOLLS
FORMERLY CURATE OF HAWORTH YORKSHIRE
WHO DIED AT THE HILL HOUSE BANAGHER
DECEMBER 2nd 1906
AGED 88
ALSO OF
MARY ANNA HIS WIFE
WHO DIED AT THE HILL HOUSE BANAGHER
FEBRUARY 27th 1915
AGED 85

The beautiful east window in the Church depicts the two Marys meeting the resurrected Christ in the Garden of Gethsemane. It was erected as a memorial to the Bell family, originally in the south transept, and moved to its present position when the church was restored in 1959.

The legend reads:

To the glory of God and in loving memory
of Rev Alan Bell, LLD born 1789 died 1839
and of Harriette his wife born 1801 died 1902
and their five sons

Alan born 1824 died 1868, James born 1826 died 1891, Arthur born 1828 died 1869 Joseph born 1831 died 1891 and William born 1839 died 1870 and of their daughters Susan born 1823 died 1844 and Frances born 1835 died 1850 and also of Surgeon Major Arthur Bell born 1840 died 1899 also of Rev Arthur Bell Nicholls of The Hill House Banagher born 1818 died 1906.

Arthur's wife, Mary Anna, did not die until 1915. It seems a pity her name was not subsequently added to the window erected for her family.

All the major newspapers published obituaries to Arthur, mainly giving a brief outline of his life, the most personal being the *Yorkshire Post* of Wednesday, 5th December, 1906, which quoted the words of Clement Shorter – 'He was a man whom any woman might revere and I was pleased to feel as I did, that here before me was the man who brought a little gleam of sunshine and happiness into the home and life of one of our greatest novelists.'

Arthur's estate was valued at £4,225.14s.2d and estate duty was paid of £123.7s.8d.[1] About six months after Arthur's death Horsfall Turner asked Mary Anna if she would sell some items to the Halifax, Bradford or Haworth Museums. She preferred Haworth and, on the understanding they were to go to the Brontë Society, sold eight items, including the plaster medallion of Branwell, for £17.4s.0d.[2] The next year many more items were put up for sale at Sotheby's. The catalogue included books and manuscripts, personal items previously owned by Charlotte, such as her writing desk and paint box, Patrick Brontë's guns and nine of the little books that had been so cherished by Arthur, six by Charlotte, three by Branwell.[3] The sale realised £718.2s.0d. In 1914 Mary again sold items at Sotheby's, this time some pieces of furniture brought by Arthur from Haworth, more books and manuscripts, including a pencil fragment of Charlotte's unfinished story, *Emma*, and a further fifteen of the little books.[4] This time £613.14s.0d. was raised.

On her death in 1915 she left to the Brontë Society: a book of French exercises written by Charlotte, a piece of her wedding wreath, two glass ink-bottles and Emily's china mug.[5] The next year, at another sale, Arthur's signet ring, containing a lock of Charlotte's hair, a book of French poetry given to her by M.

Heger on the day she left Brussels and more books and manuscripts were sold.[6]

Charlotte's wedding dress, which Arthur had cherished, she gave to his niece, Charlotte Brontë Nicholls, with instructions that she should burn it before she died. The dress was duly burnt in 1954 but it had been seen by Miss Nicholls' niece, Margaret Ross, who was able to describe it and enable the Brontë Museum to make a replica.[7]

Several years after Arthur's death two paintings by Branwell were discovered on top of a wardrobe. Mary Anna was by this time an invalid confined to her own room upstairs. It became necessary for her to have a nurse in residence and the only communicating room was Arthur's dressing room, which until this time had been kept exactly as he left it. It was while this room was being prepared that the paintings came to light. One was the so-called Pillar Portrait, which showed the three Brontë sisters with Branwell painted out in the centre, and a small head and shoulders portrait in profile of Emily.

Mary could not decide what should be done with them so she sent for her niece, Miss F. E. Bell, to ask her advice. They talked it over and eventually sent them to Reginald Smith of Smith Elder & Co., Charlotte's publishers, for his opinion. Now they both hang in the National Gallery. It is believed that the portrait of Emily was cut from another group of the three girls and Branwell. Arthur thought the painting badly executed and Emily's likeness the only one which bore much resemblance to the sitter. The rest of the picture was so poor he had it destroyed. According to some sources he gave the fragment to Martha Brown and it was returned to him after her death. He did not particularly like the larger portrait. It had not been on display but had remained folded up since his arrival at the house.

The Bell family continued to own The Hill House until the death of Major Arthur Bell in 1944. It was then sold to St. Paul's Church for use as the Rectory, but the Rectors thought it inconvenient and moved to a more modern bungalow. The house has been much altered and extended over the years. It is now in private hands.

Appendix I

Joseph Grant, B.A., Oxon, was born at Lynn, Norfolk. The same age as Arthur, he was curate to Haworth with special responsibility for Oxenhope. He was appointed Headmaster of Haworth Grammar School to replace William Ramsbottom, who was considered unsuitable because he was a Wesleyan. Grant lived at Marshlands, a house built against the School, which actually is not in Haworth, but in Marsh, part of Near Oxenhope. The building is still there. He was a friend of Arthur Nicholls, who stayed at Marsh when visiting Haworth during the period of his 'exile' at Kirk Smeaton and prior to his wedding with Charlotte Brontë. Grant and his wife Sarah were guests at the Parsonage for the wedding breakfast and again for tea after the couple's return from honeymoon. When Oxenhope was made a separate parish and a new church, St Mary the Virgin, was consecrated in 1849, he became the first incumbent. He remained there until his death in 1879.

Appendix II

Sutcliffe Sowden B.A., Magdalen College, Cambridge, was ordained by the Bishop of Ripon as a Deacon on 5th January, 1840, and as a priest on 10th January, 1841. In May, 1841, he was appointed to St James Church, Mytholmroyd, in the Calder Valley. Later that year he moved up the valley to be the incumbent of Hebden Bridge, where he remained until his death 20 years later. Quiet and rather shy, he enjoyed walking and was a keen geologist. He was a friend of the Brontës before Arthur came and used to go walking with Branwell when the latter was at Luddenden Foot. He often helped out at Haworth and after Arthur's arrival in 1845 they quickly became friends. He supplied a fulsome reference to the USPG when Arthur was thinking of becoming a missionary. He conducted the wedding of Arthur and Charlotte. When Sir James Kay-Shuttleworth asked Arthur to recommend someone for the living at Habergham, he put forward Sutcliffe's name. He was present at Patrick Brontë's funeral and he himself was drowned only two months later in a tragic accident, 8th August, 1861. There is a memorial to him in Hebden Bridge Church and a poem was written in his memory.

Appendix III

Sir James Kay-Shuttleworth 1804-77

Born James Phillips Kay, son of a Rochdale cotton manufacturer, he studied medicine in Edinburgh. A fellow pupil, Darwin, who left the course and went to Cambridge, later expressed high regard for his ability. He practised in Manchester from 1827 until 1835, then turned to government service. He became an Assistant Poor Law Commissioner and in 1839 Secretary of the Committee of Council, virtually the forerunner of the Department of Education. The department started with a budget of £20,000 and by the time he left ten years later it had reached £100,000. He had previously taken an interest in methods of teaching on the Continent, with Fellenberg and Wherli, in Switzerland, Father Gerard of Fribourg and also in the methods of David Stow of Glasgow for training teachers. James Kay distilled the best from these sources and instituted teacher training colleges and school inspectors and through these influenced the curriculum. He worked effectively and forcefully and education in this country made major advances. Matthew Arnold, who was a school inspector as well as an author, described him as the founder of public education in England. However, in 1849 he had to retire due to poor health and, for his services, was given a baronetcy. In 1842 he had married Janet Shuttleworth, an heiress, and adopted her name . Through her he obtained the house and estate of Gawthorpe Hall which brought in an income of £10,000 a year. He settled to the life of the landed gentry and employed Sir Charles Barry to make improvements to the house. Sir James had aspirations as an author and wrote two novels, *Scarsdale* in 1860 and *Ribblesdale* in 1874. He moved in literary circles and in 1850 he invited Charlotte Brontë, whom he had met in London, to Gawthorpe and later to his house in the Lake District where he introduced her to Mrs Gaskell. From 1853 his wife spent her time away from Gawthorpe travelling round the English and Continental health resorts with a Miss Poplawski, a Prussian governess as companion.

Appendix IV

Richard Monckton Milnes, Lord Houghton.
The Milnes family made their money in textile manufacturing in Wakefield. It was said that in the late 18th century they had the contract to clothe all the Russian armies. Richard Slater Milnes, who married the co-heiress of a Leeds merchant, bought the Fryston estate in 1788 and moved into the restored and extended Hall in 1790. He was a Member of Parliament for York. He was succeeded by his son, Robert Pemberton Milnes, who in 1806 was elected Member of Parliament for Pontefract. In 1808 he married the Honourable Maria Monckton, second daughter of Viscount Galway. Their son, Richard Monckton Milnes, was born in 1809. He was educated at Trinity College, Cambridge. He became Member of Parliament for Pontefract in 1837 and held the seat until 1863 when he was created 1st Baron Houghton. He married the Hon. Annabel Crewe, daughter of Baron Crewe, in 1851. He was a Fellow of the Royal Society, a Trustee of the British Museum and held many other distinguished posts. He was a poet and biographer, his major work being *The Life, Letters and Literary Remains of Keats*. During his time Fryston Hall became a meeting place for his wide circle of distinguished literary and political friends, which included Thackeray, Tennyson and Disraeli. One of the attractions of Fryston Hall was his large and select library. This included the first collection of works by de Sade and items by other pornographic writers. These were later sold to the British Museum Library. Fryston Hall was demolished in 1935, although part of the Park remains. J. Pope-Hennessy wrote a two-volume biography published by Constable, 1950-52.

His son, the second Lord Houghton, later Viscount Crewe, was the first President of the Brontë Society.

Appendix V

Cuba House

From the plan it would appear that it was originally intended that the main entrance would be on the south front opening into a substantial hall in the centre; to the right was a circular space for a staircase. This, however, was never completed and the door in the west front became the main entrance. Again according to the plan this opened directly into the large room in the north-west corner of the house. This had been partitioned off, resulting in the high narrow passageway mentioned by Charlotte. The passage led straight across the building giving access to all the rooms and ending in the staircase in the middle of the east side.

We spoke to Miss Valerie Landon, who had lived there until 1933. She said there was still no electricity or gas and the family used oil-lamps. As there was only the one staircase her mother was very worried about the risk of fire. The rooms on the ground floor were very large. As you came in the door the room to the left was the drawing room and that to her right her father's study. Further down the corridor on the right was the dining room, (the intended entrance hall). The kitchen was in the north-east corner and several smaller rooms in the south-east corner where the circular staircase should have been. The bedrooms were large but some had been divided up. There were attics and the cellars were used for storage. As a child she used to be scared of going into the 'dungeons'. Past the house, at the bottom of the grounds, there were tennis courts, and they played badminton in the former schoolroom.

Charlotte said their bedroom was a 'great room' downstairs. We do not know which room it was but it may have been the one which was later the study. The coach house and schoolroom buildings were to the east side of the house.

Appendix VI

Church Reform by Patrick Brontë

In Haworth, a parish of ancient renown,
Some preach in their surplice and others in their gown;
Other some with due hatred of tower and steeple,
Without surplice or gown hold forth to the people.
And "High Church" and "Low Church" and no church at all
'Twould trouble the brain of St Peter and St Paul –
The Parson an old man but hotter than old,
Of late in reforming had grown very bold,
And in his fierce zeal, as report loudly tells
Through legal resort had reformed the bells –
His curate who follows – with all due regard
Though foiled by the church has reformed the church yard.
Then let all schismatics look on in mute wonder;
Nor e'er dream the Church, shall in terror knock under;
'Twill go on reforming what e'er be their clatter
Till cleansed is the outside, both cup and platter –
The dead all deserted, their ghosts heavy moan
Oft shakes to the centre each slumbering stone –
The females all routed have fled with their clothes
To stackyards and brickyards; where no one knows –
And loudly have sworn by the suds which they swim in
They'll wring off his head for his warring with women,
Whilst their husbands combine and roar out in their fury,
They'll lynch him at once, without trial by jury,
But saddest of all the fair maidens declare,
Of marriage or love he must ever despair.

Glossary

ABN	Arthur Bell Nicholls
CB	Charlotte Brontë – later Charlotte Bell Nicholls
ECG	Elizabeth Clegg Gaskell
EN	Ellen Nussey
GS	George Smith, Smith Elder & Co, CB's Publisher
TWR	Thomas Wemyss Reid
WSW	William Smith Williams, CB's Editor

Berg	Berg Collection of English and American Literature, The New York Public Library, Astor Lenox and Tilden Foundations
BPM	The Brontë Society, Brontë Parsonage Museum
Brotherton	The Brotherton Collection, Leeds University Library
BST	Brontë Society Transactions
C & P	From *The Letters of Mrs Gaskell*, Edited by J. A. V. Chapple and Arthur Pollard, 1997 Mandolin, Manchester University Press, Manchester, UK
L & D	John Lock and Canon W. Dixon, *Man of Sorrow, The Life Letters and Times of Patrick Brontë*, (Nelson, 1965)
John Murray	Smith Elder & Co. archives
NRM	National Railway Museum
Pforzheimer	The Carl H. Pforzheimer Collection of Shelley & his Circle, The New York Public Library, Astor, Lenox & Tilden Foundations
Pierpont	Pierpont Morgan Library, New York
PR	Parish Registers
W & S	T. J. Wise & A. J. Symington, *The Lives, Friendships and Correspondence of the Brontë Family*, (Shakespeare Head Press. 1932)

Chapter Notes

Chapter 1

1. ABN. in old age, recalled by Helen Dillon, d. of Rev. J. J. Sharrard, Rector of Banagher, 1885-1917. *Daily Telegraph Magazine* 7.12.73 – *Supplanting Mr Rochester by* Selina Hastings.
2. CB to EN Boxing Day 1854. BPM MS BS 97.
3. The Death Certificate of Arthur Nicholls shows his age in 1906 as 87 giving a birth year of 1819. Similarly the application which he completed for the USPG shows the year of his birth as 1819. Even so his year of birth is often referred to as 1818 and his age as 88 which is shown on his gravestone.
4. Nicholls Family – BPM.
5. Bell Family Tree: – St Paul's Church, Banagher. – ABN's papers BPM MS 244.
6. Annemarie Hogan, *Banagher Royal School*, unpublished MS, Banagher Public Library.
7. Valentine Trodd, *Banagher on the Shannon*, A Historical Guide to the Town. Published privately, 1985.
8. Bodleian Library, Oxford.

Chapter 2

1. *Cornhill Magazine.* July 1910. Article by C. Holmes Cautley – *Haworth folk who knew the Brontës – Old Village Sportsman.*
2. CB to Mrs Rand 26.5.1845 Pierpont MSS2696.
3. CB to EN 18.6.1845 W & S Letter 202.
4. Hymn Sheet BPM BS x H.
5. Ordination Papers P.Eggleston Ripon Dioc. Leeds Archives RD/RO/1/1
6. James W. Stephenson, *The House of Dawson – descendants of Francis Dawson, 1786-1866, of Rise, Yorkshire.* 1950. unpublished. By permission of Mrs Jean Blackburn.
7. Tom and Cordelia Stamp, *William Scoresby, Arctic Scientist.* Caedmon of Whitby Press 1993.
8. ABN. Copy Memorandum and Account BPM VII.
9. As 1.
10,11,12   Biographical Notice, 1850 on publication of a reprint of Emily and Anne's books.

Chapter 3

1. CB to EN 10.7.1846. BPM MS Grolier E 10.
2. Rushbearing: At one time, a festival when rushes used on the church floor were changed annually. A commemoration of this practice.
3. CB to EN 17.11.46. BPM MS Grolier E12.
4. Haworth PR Bradford Archive.
5. St Paul's Denholme Gate, PR and records.
6. CB to EN 29.6.1847 W & S Letter 294.
7. CB to EN 7.10.1847 W & S Letter 308.
8. See App vi. Patrick Brontë, *Church Reform* BPM BS x H.
9. Haworth Mechanics' Institute: Kenneth Emsley, *Historic Haworth Today*, p.42 (Bradford Libraries, 1995). C. Mabel Edgerley, The Rev. Arthur Bell Nicholls, (BST part LII No 3 Vol. X).
10. CB to EN 28.4.1848 BPM MS Bonnell 201.
11. CB to EN 28.7.1848 BPM MS Grolier G14.
12. PR St Paul's, Denholme Gate.
13. CB to WSW 2.10.1848 Pierpont MSS 2696.
14. J. Grant – see appendix I.
15. Although the stethoscope, invented in 1816, was in general use in towns by this time the description by EN seems to imply it was still somewhat of a novelty in rural areas.
16. CB to EN 16.5.1849 W & S 443.

Chapter 4

1. Wills and Administrations used to be a matter for the Church Courts of Archdeacons, Bishops and Archbishops. In 1858 this was taken over by the civil authorities and the Principal Probate Registry (with District Offices) was set up. Now known as the Principal Registry of the Family Division.
2. Petition requesting the General Board of Health to send an inspector. 222 signatories.
3. Mr Atkinson of Leeds – CB's cashbook, BPM MS BS22.
4. CB to EN 19.1.50 W & S 519.
5. Sir James Kay-Shuttleworth – see Appendix III.
6. CB to EN 14.9.1850 W & S 599.
7. CB to EN 21.5.1851 W & S 668.
8. William Wood quoted in *Literary Hearthstones* by Marian Harlan.
9. CB to PB 26.6.1851 BPM BS MS 81.6.
10. CB to PB 2.6.1852 Pierpont MSS MA2696.

Chapter 5

1. CB to EN 15.12.1852 Berg.
2. CB to EN 2.1.1853 BPM MS Law Colln P3.
3. *Ibid.*

4. CB to EN 18.12.1852 Berg.
5. USPG Archives, Partnership House, 157 Waterloo Rd. London.
6. PB to CB 19.1.1853 BPM MS196.
7. PB as Flossy to CB January 1853 BPM MS197.
8. CB to EN 6.4.1853 BPM MS Grolier E23.
9. CB to EN 16.5.1853 W & S 846.
10. Nicholls' watch is now in BPM.
11. CB to EN 27.5.1853 BPM MS Grolier E25.

Chapter 6

1. J. Grant – See Appendix I.
2. *Ibid.*
3. *St Peter's Church Kirk Smeaton* by H. Robinson (1984).
4. Richard Monckton Milnes – See appendix iv.
5. ECG to Monckton Milnes 29.10.1853 C & P Letter 168.
6. Monckton Milnes to ECG 30.1.1854, Houghton Library, Harvard.
7. CB to ECG 1854 W & S 889.
8. ECG to Monckton Milnes 20.4.1854 C & P Letter 189.
9. ECG to Monckton Milnes June 1854 C &P Letter 204.
10. CB to GS 10.1.1853 BPM MS SG88 p1.
11. CB to EN 11.4.1854 MS Pforzheimer P3.
12. *Ibid.*
13. *Ibid.*
14. CB to GS 25.4.1854 BPM MS SG 90.
15. CB to MW 12.4.1854 W & S Letter 887.
16. C. Winkworth – E Shaen 8.5.1854 W & S letter 896.
17. CB. to EN 7.6.1854 W & S Letter 900.
18. CB Marriage Settlement 24.5.1854 MS BPM BSxB.
19. CB to MW 16.6.1854 W & S Letter 903.
20. Sutcliffe Sowden – See Appendix II.
21. Account by John Robinson – Love story of Charlotte Brontë – *Keighley News* 27.10.1923 p8.

Chapter 7

1. Although the different railway lines were owned by different companies, a system of through booking had come into being as early as 1842. NRM York.
2. Exhibit NRM York.
3. Bradshaw's 1854 NRM York.
4. Robert Stephenson built the railway bridge at Conway, and its larger sister at Menai, the trains running through two large, wooden-lined, steel tubes. In effect a large box girder bridge. Opened 1848/1850.
5 & 6. Letter ABN to unknown correspondent, 10/8/1903 BPM MS BS 285.75 (recently acquired.)
7. R. J. W. Selleck. *James K. Shuttleworth – Journey of an Outsider* . Woburn Press.

8. The Legend had been brought to Beddgelert as a tourist attraction in the early 1800's by David Prichard, the first Landlord of the Goat Hotel. – *Beddgelert* by Anita Pierce, Gwynedd Council and Beddgelert Historical Society, 1996.

9. The term 'packet' or 'packet boat' came into use in Elizabethan times when the Queen had special boats built to carry her packets, (correspondence) fast and reliably, particularly to and from Ireland. Has come to mean a boat carrying mails as well as passengers.

10. In 1852 a child was killed on the extension line indulging in this practice, but it was not until 1855, the year after their visit, that notices were posted on the carriages asking passengers not to encourage the children in their dangerous sport. *The Chester and Holyhead Railway* by P. E. Baughan.

11. Kingstown, now Dun Laoghaire, harbour was built in the early 19th century on the south east side of Dublin Bay to avoid having to negotiate the treacherous sandbanks near the mouth of the Liffey. Named Kingstown in honour of George IV who sailed from the new harbour in 1821.

12. Renamed after Queen Victoria landed here in 1849.

13. The Grand Canal proposed by Parliament in 1715, built 1756-1796 to link Dublin with the Shannon, giving the longest waterway in the British Isles. Enters the Shannon at Shannon Harbour just north of Banagher.

14. CB to MW 10.7.1854 W & S Letter 905.

15. Cuba Court – see Appendix V.

16. Kilkee is in a low-lying horse-shoe-shaped sandy bay which opens out at the two ends. It is from here that the cliffs begin to rise up. West End Hotel, no longer in existence, was on the south side of the bay at the point where the sands gave way to cliffs. There are large rocky outcrops on to the beach and it would be here that they sat and watched the 'broad Atlantic foaming at our feet'.

17. CB to Catherine Wooler 18.7.1854 W & S Letter 906.

18. ABN to George Sowden 10.8.1854 BPM MS 247.

19. CB to Catherine Winkworth 27.7.1854 Brotherton.

20. Collection is now in BPM.

21. The Gap of Dunloe is a wild and deep ravine in Killarney separating the mountains, Mcgillycuddy's Reeks and the Purple Mountain. There is a stream and several lakes. Famous for its savage beauty.

22. The apparition was probably caused by the phenomenon of the sun casting their shadows on the mist, similarly to the well known 'Spectre of Brocken' in Germany.

23. As 19.

24. CB to Martha Brown 28.7.1854 BPM MS 96.

Chapter 8

1. CB to MW 22.8.1854 W & S Letter 913.

2. Charlotte probably made little of this incident as it seems likely she

destroyed Ellen's letters as soon as she had dealt with the contents. If not, she had either destroyed or hidden them before her marriage as Arthur later claimed he never found any.

3. EN to ABN. Nov.1854 W & S Letter 922.
4. CB to EN 9.8.1854 W & S 910.
5. CB to EN 21.11.1854 MS Berg.
6. CB to EN 29.11.1854 W & S Letter 927.
7. CB to EN 26.12.1854 BPM MS BS97.
8. CB to EN 19.1.1855 BPM MS BS99.

Chapter 9

1. *Cornhill Magazine* July 1910 article by C. Holmes Cautley, Haworth Folk who knew the Brontës – Old Village Sportsman.
2. CB to EN 29.11.1854 W & S 927.
3. CB to EN 7.12.1854 BPM MS Grolier E3O.
4. CB to EN 26.12.1854 BST 16.18.1919.
5. CB to EN 19.1.1855 BPM MS BS99.
6. ABN to EN 14.2.1855 Brotherton.
7. CB to Amelia Taylor Feb 1855 BPM BS MS103.
8. Last Will & Testament CB 17.2.1885 Borthwick Institute, York.
9. CB to Laetitia Wheelwright 15.2.1855 W & S 943.
10. CB to EN 21.2.1855 BPM MS 101.
11. Mrs Ellis H.Chadwick, *In the Footsteps of the Brontës* (Pitman & Sons, 1914).
12. Mrs Gaskell, *The life of Charlotte Brontë*, Smith Elder & Co. 1857.
13. L & D p 477.
14. ABN to EN 31.3.1855. BPM MS 247.
15. EN to GS 1.6.1860 John Murray.
16. *Ibid.*
17. L & D. p.477.
18. Copy Death certificate CBN 31.3.1855 BPM.

Chapter 10

1. *Daily News* 6.4.1855 – Harriette Martineau, Obituary of CB.
2. EN to ABN 6.6.1855 W & S 954.
3. *Sharpes London Magazine* June 1855.
4. ABN to EN 11.6.1855 W & S 955.
5. PB to ECG 16.6.1855 W & S 956 (dated 16.7.1855).
6. PB to ECG 16.6.1855 BST 8.43.87-8.
7. ECG to EN 24.7.1855 C & P 257.
8. ABN to EN 24.7.1855 Brotherton.
9. PB to ECG 23.1.1856 BST 8.43.97.
10. See appendix iii Sir James Kay-Shuttleworth.
11. Pierpont MS *The Professor.*
12. ABN to GS 28.11.1856 John Murray.

13. ABN to GS 1.12.1856 John Murray.
14. ECG to GS 11.12.1856 C & P 322.
15. ABN to GS 2.4.1857 John Murray.

Chapter 11

1. Correspondence re Clergy School, Cowan Bridge April-August 1857 in *The Daily News*, *The Leeds Mercury* and *The Halifax Guardian*, W & S Appendix i.
2. *Bradford Observer* – August September 1857.
3. ABN to Harriet Martineau 14.11.1857 John Murray.
4. ABN to GS 23.12.1859 John Murray.
5. *Bradford Observer* 9.8.1860.
6. Bradford Archives, Haworth PR.
7. *Halifax Courier* 21.7.1860.
8. ABN to Monckton Milnes 21.12.1860 Trinity College, Cambridge.
9. Meta Gaskell to friend 5.11.1860 W & S 1007.

Chapter 12

1. Last Will and Testament PB 20.6.1855.
2. *Halifax Guardian* 10.8.1861 Obituary Sutcliffe Sowden.
3. *Cornhill Magazine*. July 1910, article by C. Holmes Cautley, 'Haworth folk who knew the Brontës'. Old Village Sportsman.
4. MS Heaton A548, WYAS Bradford.
5. Sotheby's Catalogue, 1916 sale lot 670.
6. John Cragg, auctioneer Bill of sale 1 & 2.10.1861. BPM BSX.

Chapter 13

1. Dr Ingham – the Haworth doctor who had attended Charlotte in her last illness.
2. ABN to Martha Brown 33 letters 1861-1880 BPM MSS BS 250 – 283.
3. *Banagher on Shannon* – Valentine Trodd 1985.
4. Marriage Cert. ABN to Mary Anna Bell.

Chapter 14

1. Mrs Ellis H.Chadwick, *In the Footsteps of the Brontës* (Pitman, 1914).
2. Thesis on *Banagher Royal School* by Annemarie Hogan, unpublished MS Banagher Public Library.
3. ABN to Martha Brown 24.9.1868 BPM MS BS271.
4. Reminiscences by Ethel Selkirk from *The Irish Times* c.1955 BST:15:79:345.
5. *Guardian Weekly* 2 October 1995. Article by F. E. Bell, (then aged 92,

niece of Mary Anna Bell), 'Charlotte Brontë's Irish Relations'.
6. *Yorkshire Weekly Post* 1st January 1927 article by H. K. Bell, nephew of ABN, 'Charlotte Brontë's Husband in Later Life'.
7. As 4.
8. As 6.
9. *Daily Telegraph Magazine*, 7 December 1973. Recollections of Helen Dillon from *Supplanting Mr Rochester* by Selina Hastings.
10. *Cornhill Magazine*, Jan 1927. *Charlotte Brontë's Husband* by H. K. Bell.
11. *That Vandal Wade* by Michael Baumber BST Vol.22 1997.
12. Copy of letter – ABN to Rev. Wade 22.4.1879 BPM MS BS VII.
13. S. Biddell to EN 20.7.1881 BPM MS Cadman XIV G2.
14. S. Biddell to EN 27.3.1882 BPM MS Cadman XIV G7.

Chapter 15

1. The Letters of Charlotte Brontë p.34 M.Smith Clarendon Press 1995.
2. GS to EN 18.1.1869 BPM MS Cadman B6.
3. GS to EN 21.1.1869 BPM MS Cadman B7.
4. EN to GS? undated BPM MS Cadman B10.
5. GS to EN 12.2.1869 BPM MS Cadman B9.
6. GS to EN 24.2.1869 BPM MS Cadman B11.
7. EN to GS 27.2.1869 BPM MS Cadman B12.
8. EN to TWR 10.5.1876 MS Berg.
9. TWR to EN 2.11.1876 BPM Cadman E12.
10. ABN to TWR 6.11.1876 MS Berg.
11. EN to TWR 3.11.1876 MS Berg.
12. TWR to EN 8.3.1877 BPM MS Cadman E16.
13. Rev. A. E.Wilkes to EN 2.6.1882 BPM MS Cadman F5.
14. Rev. R. J. Ridley to C.K.Shorter W & S Vol.iv p289.
15. W. Wright to EN 24.2.1891 BPM MS Cadman S1.
16. W. Wright to EN 27.2.1891 BPM MS Cadman S3.
17. EN to G. Armytage 9.11.1892 MS WYAS Calderdale, Halifax.
18. Clement Shorter, *CB and Her Circle*, (Hodder & Stoughton,1896).
19. *Ibid.*
20. Copy of agreement. BPM.
21. CB to MW 16.6.1854 W & S 903.

Chapter 16

1. Valentine Trodd, *Midlanders, Chronicle of a Midland Parish*, (Scéal Publications, Banagher, 1994) pp.187-188.
2. *Ibid* pp.101-102.
3. ABN to Clement Shorter 24.6.1895. MS Brotherton.
4. ABN to Clement Shorter 21.1.1896. MS Brotherton.
5. ABN to Clement Shorter 26.4.1895. MS Brotherton.
6. ABN to Clement Shorter 22.5.1895. MS Brotherton.
7. ABN to Clement Shorter 8.12.1897. MS Brotherton.

8. ABN to Clement Shorter 13.10.1896. MS Brotherton.
9. ABN to W. T. Field 12.3.1895. BPM MS BS 284.
10. W. T. Field to Clement Shorter 13.4.1899 MS Brotherton.
11. ABN to Clement Shorter 3.2.1900. MS Brotherton.
12. ABN to W. T. Field 28.1.1902 BPM BS 285.
13. Will ABN BPM.
14. Mary Anna Nicholls to W. T. Field. Letter read by him at Brontë Society 1905 Commemoration Meeting. BS MS VII.

Aftermath

1. Probate and photo copy of will of A. B. Nicholls BPM XA.
2. Mary Anna Nicholls to W. T. Field 30.3.1907 & 7.4.1907 BPM MS XII.
3. Sotheby's Catalogue 26 & 27 July 1907.
4. *loc. cit.* 29 July 1914.
5. BST Vol. 15 1919.
6. *Yorkshire Observer,* Saturday 16 December 1916.
7. *Yorkshire Post,* 19 June 1967.

A Select Bibliography

The Brontë Family:
Brontë Society Transactions (formerly Publications) contain a wealth of articles and lectures since the inception of the society.
Elizabeth C. Gaskell: *The Life of Charlotte Brontë*, (Smith Elder & Co. 1857 first and third (revised) editions). There is a Penguin Classics edition 1985 edited by Alan Shelston.
Clement K. Shorter: *Charlotte Brontë and Her Circle*, (Hodder and Stoughton, 1896); *The Brontës, Life and Letters*, (Scribners New York, 1908. Reprinted by Haskell House 1969).
Ellis H. Chadwick: *In the Footsteps of the Brontës*, (Pitman, 1914).
Margaret Lane: *The Brontë Story*, (William Heinemann, 1953).
John Lock and Canon W. Dixon: *Man of Sorrow*, (Nelson 1965).
Winifred Gerin: *Charlotte Brontë*, (Oxford University Press, 1967).
Margot Peters: *Unquiet soul*, (Hodder & Stoughton, 1975).
Juliet Barker: *The Brontës*, (Phoenix, 1995, first published Weidenfeld and Nicolson, 1994).

Letters:
T. J. Wise & A. J. Symington: *The Lives Friendships and Correspondence of the Brontë Family*, (Shakespeare Head Press, 1932).
Margaret Smith: *The Letters of Charlotte Brontë*, Vol 1 1829-1847, (Clarendon Press, Oxford, 1995).
Juliet Barker: *The Brontës: A Life in Letters*, (Viking, 1997).
J. A. V. Chapple and Arthur Pollard: *The Letters of Mrs Gaskell*, (Mandolin,1997, first published Manchester University Press, 1966).

Other:
Mabel Ferrett: *The Taylors of the Red House, Kirklees* (Metropolitan Council, 1987).

Kenneth Emsley: *Historic Haworth Today*, (Bradford Libraries, 1995).

Charles Lemon: *A Centenary History of the Brontë Society 1893-1993*, (The Brontë Society, 1993); *Early Visitors to Haworth*, (The Brontë Society, 1996).

Valentine Trodd: *Banagher on the Shannon, A Historical Guide to the Town*, (Published by local Subscription, 1985); *Midlanders, Chronicle of a Midland Parish*, (Scéal Publications, 1994).

Tom and Cordelia Stamp: *William Scoresby, Arctic Explorer*, (Caedmon of Whitby Press, 1993, first published 1976).

Harry Robinson: *St Peter's Church, Kirk Smeaton*, (1984).

R. J. W. Sellick: *James Kay-Shuttleworth, Journey of an Outsider*, (Woburn Press).

Anita Pierce: *Beddgelert*, (Gwynedd Council and Beddgelert Historical Society, 1996).

P. E. Baughan: *The Chester and Holyhead Railway*.

INDEX